how to start a home-based

House Painting Business

how to start a home-based

House Painting Business

Deborah Bouziden

Guilford, Connecticut

Editorial Director: Cynthia Hughes Cullen
Editor: Tracee Williams
Text Design: Sheryl P. Kober
Layout: Sue Murray

ISSN 2163-8780
ISBN 978-0-7627-7203-2

Printed in the United States of America
10 9 8 7 6 5 4 3 2 1

I would like to dedicate this book first of all to my husband, David. Secondly, to his brothers, Tom and Terry, brother-in-law, Whitey, and his dad, Delore, and uncles, Richard, Tom, and Jim, all of whom are or were house painters. Thirdly, to the rest of the painters out there who also add color to our world, one wall at a time.

Contents

Acknowledgments

In putting together a book like this, there are always more people involved than just the author. I would like to thank first of all my husband, David, who answered all my painting and painting-business questions with patience, no matter how many times I asked them. Secondly, our support team, Jane Haskin, our banker, and Jean Sharp, her vice president; Hazel Boone, our accountant; Jason Hicks, our attorney; Donna, our go-to girl for all things insurance related; and our crew, Nathan, Bob, and Marvel.

I would also like to thank all the house painters who got back to me with answers to my questions and took the time to tell me what makes their house painting businesses successful.

Finally, I would be remiss if I didn't thank my editors, Cynthia Hughes and Tracee Williams, for making the book come together and for making my words look better on the published page than they did in the rough draft.

Introduction

According to David Bouziden, president and owner of Freedom Painting Service Inc. and my husband, house painting is the cheapest and fastest way to make money of all the service jobs out there. Why?

"All you need is a paintbrush and roller to get started," David says.

He should know. He's been in the painting business for more than forty-five years. As a teenager, his original career plan was to become an accountant, and he was taking classes for that very purpose. But then he found he could make more money painting, so his career choice was set. Starting at the age of seventeen working with his uncle and dad, he learned the business toiling in the trenches. His first jobs were prep work like sanding, caulking, and puttying walls on residential houses.

After mastering a paintbrush and roller, he struck out on his own and in the mid- to late '70s worked for contractor A. J. Penney painting houses. Through this experience he expanded his skills, learning how to stain wood and seal it, spray acoustic ceilings, do specialty walls, and work on different surfaces like stucco, metal, concrete, and brick. When Penney decided to retire, David, on the advice of a personal friend and financier, took on two partners and started Freedom Painting Service Inc. in 1980.

At first, their primary source of income was house painting, but over the years their business expanded into commercial work. While they still painted houses, primarily new ones, their commercial workload became so large, growing to include out-of-state work, that in 1993, the three partners split. David kept ownership of Freedom Painting Service, and the other two partners started companies of their own. At that time, too, I became secretary and treasurer of the company.

Freedom Painting Service has worked on jobs in Minnesota, Texas, New Mexico, Colorado, Kansas, and Oklahoma, at such job sites as prisons, hotels, Federal Reserves, Air Force bases, courthouses, dentist offices, and hospitals. While David has painted houses with a crew of one, he has also run big jobs with a ten-man crew. Freedom Painting Service has been listed on Dun & Bradstreet as having more than $1 million in annual contract paintwork. David took on another partner in 2005, his son Nathan. Today, Freedom Painting Service works in Colorado and Oklahoma doing commercial jobs as well as the occasional house.

Over the years, David has seen and experienced it all. In the early years of his career, he made mistakes in the direction he wanted to take his business and whom he hired to work with and for him. He spent a lot of time reinventing the wheel as it were. He watched as others tried to break into house painting and grew too big too fast and then watched as their businesses collapsed around them. He watched another house painter buy new trucks and new equipment, take on too many loans and too much work, and then suffer a massive heart attack from the stress. While our banker has been with us from the beginning, we weren't sure at first whether we needed an accountant until we got audited or an attorney until we needed to sue. We've learned a great many lessons over the years, and through the pages of this book, we've tried to impart those thirty-plus years of experience, hardships, and hard lessons learned. At the very least, we'll raise a red flag when problems occur that you need to stop and think about, a yellow flag when caution needs to be taken, and a green flag when it's full throttle ahead.

David believes there will always be a need for his profession. Homes and other buildings are always being built, bought, and sold. Improvements and upgrades are standard in our society, and who better to call than a painter for a fresh coat of paint.

House painting is a service business, and during an economic slowdown, service companies tend to do better than corporate jobs, according to economists. The U.S. Bureau of Labor Statistics (BLS) stated that the number of construction jobs would grow by 19 percent through 2018. The reason is that new structures will have to be built to handle the baby boomers as they age, new housing additions will be needed for high population growth areas, and old structures will need to be either extensively renovated or torn down and rebuilt. With the rebuilding of these structures, demand for the finishing trades will be high. Because of this good house painters will always be in demand.

"People who need painters are either too busy to do the job or are not interested in doing the sometimes messy jobs themselves," David says. "They look for painters who can do the job in a timely manner, clean up after themselves, and have integrity before, during, and after the job."

The list of jobs available to the house painter is extensive. Besides changing the look on the interior of a house, clients sometimes want to spruce up the outside of their homes as well. When people get ready to sell their homes, the first thing a real estate agent will say is to get a fresh coat of paint on the walls. David has had those types of calls from real estate agents as well as calls from people who need a paint job after damage from a flood or a fire.

With more than thirty years of experience running a company, he knows the rewards, problems, and pitfalls of doing this type of work, building a business, and keeping its reputation high. When someone hires or contracts Freedom Painting Service to do a job, he knows he will get professional workmanship in the shortest amount of time; integrity and quality are two of the company's trademarks. David has hired employees and has had to let them go. He has had well-paying jobs and not-so-well-paying jobs. He has had workers' compensation claims, has had money to buy equipment and expand his business, and then has had contractors who didn't pay after a job was completed, resulting in losses of thousands of dollars. Through all this, he has learned what to do and what not to do, which jobs to take and which to avoid.

David has learned through the years that there are good times and bad times in this business. Typically the spring, summer, and fall are the busiest times of year. Winter work slows way down. His biggest frustrations are with people who will not pay or with those who, once the work is done, call back over and over asking him to "touch up" or fix scratches or walls ruined by movers, electricians, plumbers, and drywall installers.

With this experience, knowledge, and expertise, we hope to impart to you, a new entrepreneur, the wisdom to build your business through the pages of this book. Over the years, we have worked with bankers, accountants, lawyers, employees, inspectors, commissioners, contractors, and clients. By working with them, we have learned from them.

This book will not teach you how to paint, but it will offer you suggestions on how to run a painting business. It is designed to give you small bites of information instead of big gulps. Through its pages, you will explore the reasons to start a painting business, whether it is right for you, and whether you should run the business part time or jump in with both feet and go full time. We will discuss the pros and cons of this decision as well as where you can go to learn different painting techniques and skills if that is your wish.

In chapters 2 and 3, there will be information on figuring out what kind of business you want and defining the four business types available to you. We will look at the tools you need and storage facilities, and there will be checklists so you can see where you are and where you want to be with your business. Once you decide what kind of an office you want, there will be suggestions about what equipment you might need, and more importantly, we will discuss what kind of equipment you may need on your first job and thereafter.

Following chapters will cover putting together a business plan, why you need one, and what it can do for you, financial planning and management, how this business may differ from other businesses, and what to do in fat and lean financial times. There is a chapter on building your team from internal partners like bankers, attorneys, and accountants to external support like your employees, as well as a chapter on ethical, safety, and legal issues and a chapter on marketing your business. In this chapter we will discuss everything from word-of-mouth advertising to running large ads in newspapers and on billboards. We will also cover how the Internet can help you get the word out about your business.

In the appendix are valuable resources that can be found on the web, at your local brick-and-mortar bookstore, or at your favorite electronic bookstore. Here you will find contacts for places to go for help like the Small Business Administration or organizations you can join like the national painters union. If you want to expand your skills, learn faux techniques, or find out more about lead paint, the appendix lists places to do that, as well.

According to the U.S. Small Business Administration Office of Advocacy 2010 fact sheet, there were 27.5 million small businesses in the United States in 2009 with more than 552,000 small businesses opening that year alone. Running a home-based business is not easy or for the faint of heart, but it does have its rewards. Our goal for this book is to guide and point you in the direction of success. With a little forethought, planning, and hard work, you too can have a successful home-based house painting business. We wish you a busy, safe, and profitable future.

So You Want to Start a House Painting Business

Perhaps you have read or heard about the money that can be made painting houses. Perhaps you have had some experience by painting your own house or helping others paint theirs, and you realize you like holding a paintbrush in your hand. Perhaps you like the thought of running your own business, think this is a good fit for you, and are now motivated enough to pull it together and get started.

While all that is great, you have to be realistic and look at the downside, too. Are you physically fit? Will you be able to climb ladders? Carry heavy equipment? Are you willing to put in long days and work some weekends to complete jobs? How will you get jobs? What kind of jobs do you want? Are you willing to go above and beyond for the client to secure work and build up your client base? Can you afford to work steadily for nine months of the year and then not do anything during the winter?

House Painting Is a Service Business

It is important to understand exactly what kind of business you are starting. As a house painter you will not be selling paint but applying it. Many clients already know what colors they want on their walls, and if they or you are working with an architect, the specs are probably laid out. This does not mean that you don't need to know about paint and colors; you do. But just know in advance that you are offering a service not a product.

A service business is one in which you offer services to a consumer. Service companies and businesses are big all over the world, and certain service businesses continue to do well in any economic climate, good or bad.

A service business is intangible, meaning that you can't actually hold the service in your hand. The service is only required when a customer requests it and is paid for after the service is rendered. Sometimes a company will have a different branch that offers services, like a printing company that offers design services to its customers.

According to James Stephenson in his book, *202 Services You Can Sell for Big Profits*, "anyone and everyone can sell a service" because every person possesses some level of experience, knowledge, or skill that others are willing to pay for when that particular service is needed.

There are many kinds of service businesses—home health care, tutoring in the education field, and consulting in business, for example. Other service businesses include appliance repair, plumbing, housecleaning, lawn care, and yes, house painting.

The Who, What, When, Where, and Why of a House Painter's Life

So, let's get down to the nitty-gritty.

Who can be a house painter? Anyone. Man or woman. While the current workforce is predominately male, women can make strides in this field. For every one hundred pounds a man can lift, a woman can find a way to roll it. It does take strength to lift ladders, but if a person is in good health, there are really no limits to who can do this job.

The list of *what* can be painted is endless. Houses, interior and exterior, condos, apartments, garages, office complexes, medical facilities, and these are only a few to consider. As a house painter, you need to think about whether you want to paint new homes, existing ones, or remodels. By deciding which area to specialize in, you will be able to target your market for finding work.

The question of *when* to paint is an easy one. Obviously, you don't want to paint exteriors when it's raining, sleeting, or snowing because the paint will wash off or freeze. It's also best to avoid painting outdoors when the wind is gusting, especially if you are spraying. Many a painter has been sued by individuals who say that "overspray" damaged their cars. Another time not to paint—perhaps not as well known—is when the temperature drops below 35 degrees and will be at freezing for an extended period. If the interior has no heat and the temperature will be freezing, the paint job could freeze and peel off. If the job is pressing and the temperature is hovering around 35 degrees, make sure the walls dry or will be able to dry before freezing temperatures arrive. This, of course, limits the time you can paint, but this is part of the business.

Spring, summer, and fall are typically a painter's busiest times. Winter slows work down because of the freezing issues. If the job site has heat in the interior, though, you should be fine.

Painting can be done *anywhere* there is a structure that needs to be painted. One consideration is the need for a vehicle to get you to that location. A truck or van is ideal. You will need to transport paint, your equipment, and sometimes ladders, so if you own a small car or a sports car, you will have trouble fitting everything inside.

And now for the *why*s of being a house painter. I'm sure you have given much thought to owning and running your own business. If you haven't, you need to. Perhaps you are tired of a nine-to-five job, a boss telling you what to do all the time, and office politics. Just be aware that for all the negatives related to your job, there will be downsides to having your own business.

On your job now, you have set hours and a guaranteed paycheck every Friday. With your own business, you may not be able to take weekends off. You may not get paid for ten to thirty days after you have started a job. What if you take a check from someone and that check bounces? The job you have now no doubt offers insurance, pays workers' compensation, and takes out taxes. Being your own boss means you are responsible for those items yourself. Currently, you probably get sick days, holidays off, and a one- or two-week vacation. With your own business, when you aren't working, you aren't making money.

Success Stories

Dana Dawes from Idaho. "I started my own company in 1980. Starting my own company gave me the flexibility to set my own schedule and the freedom to conduct jobs the way I thought they should be done." At one time Dawes had as many as eight employees working for him. Today, he has two. He is not sorry about scaling back. "I love the freedom to take on or turn down jobs of my own choosing, and I like continuing to provide superior service to my clients."

"It was a challenge for me controlling the quality and costs associated with expansion of the business. It worked best for me to scale back the operation to its current size," Dawes adds.

If you have thought about all that and are prepared for it, starting a home-based house painting business may be right for you. You will be able to be your own boss, set your own hours, and possibly take a long vacation, if work does get slow and you have saved up some money.

The point I'm trying to make is to think this through. If you are excited and enthusiastic about a new adventure in your life, ready to work more and harder, ready to take on the risk a new business presents, then by all means get started.

Do You Have the "Right Stuff" to be a House Painter?

To take this process one step further, answer the following questions to see if you are ready to start a business of your own. Think about each question and answer honestly. No one is looking over your shoulder, telling you how you should answer or what you should think. This moment is yours. You know yourself better than anyone. Knowing your strengths can take you far, but you have to face up to your limitations as well.

When you own your own business, problems and situations will arise that you are going to have to take care of. That's the nature of business. How are you going to handle the stress that comes with those problems? How will you handle the curves in the road? Answer the following questions and see if you have the right stuff:

1. *Do you have a strong constitution and work well under pressure and stress?* If you are prone to bouts of depression or fits of anger when events aren't going your way or going smoothly, you probably should think about another line of work. Obstacles will arise. Just when you're ready to start a job, a blizzard will keep you from working for days. If you can stay calm in the midst of trouble, you will be happier and able to get more work done in the long run.

2. *Do you have a good attitude about life in general?* Being a positive and happy person will help you go far in this business. Helping people change the look of their home is a good thing. It gives them a better outlook on life, and it should make you feel good that you are helping.

3. *Do you like people?* You will be dealing with people on every job you get. You will have to deal with their idiosyncrasies, opinions, and personalities. You've got to like people so you can get along with them. If you are a curmudgeon or grouch, clients will be turned off and not recommend you for other jobs. No one likes to hear other people complain; they have their own problems.

4. *Are you a good listener?* As a service provider, your job is to give people what they want. To do that, you will need to hear what they are saying and understand what they mean. Then, you have to translate those wishes to the interior or exterior of their homes. By listening to your clients, you can provide a thorough, more complete job.

5. *Are you an independent thinker?* When you own a business, you have to *know* what to do. If you don't know, you have to be able to think for yourself and find out what that is without someone telling you. As a business owner, you're out there on your own, and you are the boss.

6. *Can you stay focused?* There will come a time when you have painted so many walls, you feel as if you are painting the same one over and over again. And now here is another wall, the same color, the same size, with the same number of windows or electrical outlets. This might lead you to become distracted, leaving that job to work on another. On this occasion, you will need to stay focused, work on that wall until it is finished, and then move on.

7. *Are you energetic?* In this line of work, you have to have the energy to put in eight- to twelve-hour days, seven-day weeks, and thirty-day months. If you are exhausted at the end of an eight-hour day, you might need to reconsider.

8. *Are you a self-starter?* You will be the one going out in the morning to start or work on the job any given day. There will be no boss telling you what to do, kicking your behind because you are late to work or don't show up at all. You are going to have to take the initiative to get out on the job *every* morning.

9. *Can you motivate yourself?* There are going to be days when you don't feel well, when you don't want to talk to clients and give bids, and when you don't feel like working. If you own a business, you are going to have to go do these tasks anyway. There are no days off. Being unproductive means no pay. You're going to have to hit the pavement, make phone calls, talk to people, and, yes, work to build your business and keep it up and running.

10. *Are you physically fit?* In this field, you will be on your feet 90 percent of your workday. You will have to climb ladders, bend over more times than you can count, reach over your head, load and unload equipment, and produce on a daily basis. This isn't an easy job, and if you're not fit for it, you could seriously injure yourself.

11. *Are you persistent?* Salesmen report it takes ten noes to get one yes. Running and operating a business is time-consuming and sometimes disheartening

when you try to get jobs and everyone says no. But don't give up. The more noes you receive, the more likely your yeses are just around the corner.

12. *Are you willing to make mistakes?* When you run your own business, you will not only make mistakes in your work area but also in your business. It is inevitable. If you want everything to run smoothly all the time, owning and running a business is not for you. Unforeseen events are going to happen. You will paint a wall, but once the paint is on, the owner or architect will want a different color. You will plan to have your money within so many days, and payment still won't arrive. Maybe you forgot to invoice. Maybe the invoice got lost in the mail. The key is to know up front that mistakes are going to be made, to accept them, and to decide you will learn from those mistakes.

So, what do you think? Did you answer yes to most of the questions? If you did, you are probably a good candidate for this line of work. Don't be discouraged if you didn't. Maybe start small and work on improving the qualities listed in the quiz. No one who starts a business begins by knowing everything. Owning and running a business is a big challenge, one you can manage if you face your shortcomings head on and commit to working on them.

The House Painter's Day

You've decided that this is the career path for you. Let's take a look at the typical day of a house painter.

You start off your morning around 6:00 a.m. If you didn't load your equipment the night before, with coffee cup in hand, you gather the tools you will need on your job today and put them in your truck or van. Heading out, you swing by the paint store to pick up your customer's paint only to find that the store hasn't mixed it or it hasn't arrived from the warehouse yet. You grab another cup of coffee, kill forty-five minutes to an hour talking to other painters and trying to decide if you need to pick up anything else while at the paint store. You finally get your paint and off you go.

About 7:30 or 8:00 a.m. you arrive at your job site. It is a new home, so you can go in and get started right away. You might have brought your portable radio or you snap on your iPod to listen to music while you work. You unload your equipment and the paint, pour another cup of coffee from your thermos, and get to work. There are doors to sand and walls to tape, putty, and prime. By 10:30 a.m., you've gotten a room ready to paint and you take a break. While on break you take a call from a client whose house you completed last week. He has some places that need patching and touching up. After the plumbers left, there were some dings on the wall and scratches in the woodwork. You tell your client that you'll be over later that day to fix his walls and then you are back to work by 10:45 a.m.

You begin to stain the doors and trim and realize the stain color you picked up this morning is too dark. It doesn't match the stain you used in the bathroom. Taking a piece of wood from the garage, you make a stain sample using the remnants of stain left in your paint can from yesterday and check to make sure it matches the bathroom color. You tap the lid on the new stain can, attempt to clean your hands, and head off to the paint store with your sample. After forty-five minutes, you have your matching stain and head back to the work site. You munch down the lunch you packed earlier that morning and start the second half of your day by rag staining and sealing more doors and trim. Interruptions happen. The builder of the house you are working on calls to let you know that the electricians are going to have to move an outlet, so if you've painted that room, you'll have to patch and paint it again when they finish. Another builder calls to tell you his house is ready, and a third calls wanting a bid on another that is just going up.

At 3:00 p.m., you start wrapping up work on this job, seal your paint cans, clean your brushes, load your equipment if the house isn't secured, and head over to fix the job the plumbers messed up.

When you arrive and inspect the damage, you are surprised to find a hole about the size of a basketball that will take more supplies than you have on your truck. You touch up the other areas throughout the house and schedule a time to return the following week.

Leaving there about 4:30 p.m., you head across town to look at another job. Carrying your tape measure and notepad, you walk through the house, measuring and making notes. You show the homeowner some paint chips and tell him to decide what colors he would like. That way you can make him a larger sample to double-check his color choice.

You make a call to one of your clients on the way home and arrive there about 6:00 p.m. After loading your equipment for the following day, you settle down to make up a few estimate sheets, one for a house you looked at the day before and one for the house you looked at today. About 8:30 p.m., you pull out a set of blueprints and start to look at them for another job. Finally, around 10:00 p.m., you call it quits and head to bed.

Tomorrow is a new day, and you will start the process over again. The weeks following may find you at another house, another job, but your routine will basically be the same.

What Kind of Work Can the House Painter Find?

The house painter is a person who specializes in painting houses, apartments, condos, and townhouses. The range of the business can be wide, from painting one wall to an entire house's interior and exterior. You can have a one-man business or hire one or several more people to help.

In this type of business, you move from job to job, finishing up one and starting another. Occasionally, you may be called back to update an old paint job at the same location. Repeat business is good. But more than likely, each new job will be a fresh location.

The work is hard and, as the owner of the business, more demanding than working for someone else, but in the end it is well worth the sacrifices you will make to get your company up and running and keep it running for years to come. While plumbers and electricians are required to be licensed by each state they work in, house painters are not under such restrictions. At times certain cities or states will require the house painter to get a permit or be bonded, but that is discretionary. You will need to contact the Department of Labor for the state you work in and the city clerk's office for the city you are working in to see if a permit or bonding is required for your area of expertise.

Although no licensing is required to paint, you may want to specialize in faux painting or restoring older houses. There are faux-painting schools that offer classes, certification, and the use of their specific products. You don't have to be an artist to do faux walls; you just have to know certain techniques. To work on houses built before 1978, you will have to be "lead abatement certified." This certification allows you to safely remove the old paint from the house, which contained lead, and apply new paint without lead. Do not neglect this certification. The current penalty for not having proper certification is $37,500 per day, per incident. To become lead certified, you must attend an Environmental Protection Agency (EPA) approved classes and pass a written test. To learn more about classes in your area contact the National Lead Information Center at (800) 424-LEAD (5323).

Going from being a regular house painter to a specialized field is a good move. It can help you make more money and offer you a change from painting the average everyday wall. Though most people start out doing the usual flat wall type of house painting, you may be interested in colors, wallpaper, or wood. You can decide at any time to specialize in these areas and continue doing your regular painting at the same time.

You may think or have been told that work for the house painter is limited. That simply isn't true. There are many places to find work if you are willing to look for it and get the word out that you are in the business of house painting. If and when you decide to specialize, your workload may increase, but then so can the price you put on your work.

In the next few pages, we will investigate different places to find work and how to get your foot in the door with these lucrative opportunities.

New Houses

Certain areas of the country are experiencing a downturn in the new-housing market because of the economy, but those same regions will still have new homes going up. Subdivisions are being built, and the new-home market will make a recovery once people start buying again.

Painting new houses is much easier in many respects than painting existing houses. In new houses, the carpeting or plumbing fixtures won't be in, so you don't have to worry about spills or taping those fixtures; you won't have to move furniture around, which will save time on the job; and usually there is no homeowner coming in and out.

Your goal should be to introduce yourself to the home builders in your area. Give them your card. Tell them you would like to give them a bid on the next home they build. Most of the time, they will already have a painter, but don't let that discourage you.

Encourage the builder to keep your card in case you are needed. Circumstances change and can change overnight. If the builder has too many houses for his regular painter to work on or if his painter becomes ill, he will have your card and may give you an opportunity to work for him.

Existing Houses

Typically these types of homes are the backbone of the house painter's existence. These homes offer opportunities for interior and exterior work. Homeowners may need their homes painted on the outside once every five years and the inside whenever the whim strikes them. Sometimes the paint job is done just to update the look of the house. At other times, the homeowner may be going for a totally different look—perhaps she wants an accent wall or an off-the-chart room color.

Also, if the homeowner decides to sell his home, the first thing his real estate agent will stress is to get a new coat of paint on the walls to freshen up the look. More times than not, the homeowner is simply too busy to tackle the job himself or doesn't want to deal with the mess that can be created by a paint job.

That's where you come in. Painting existing houses can be a pain, however. You have to watch out for breakables, move furniture (unless it's stated in your contract, furniture must be moved), and be careful not to spill any paint on the carpet or flooring.

Getting this work can be fairly straightforward and simple, however. Word of mouth is always your best advertisement, but if you are just getting started, you might want to place a small ad in your local newspaper. And don't discount real estate agents. Just as with builders of new houses, meet with real estate agents in your area, give them your card, and tell them you would appreciate it if they passed your name onto their clients. Remember, too, that real estate agents sometimes buy and flip homes. If you meet one and he needs a paint job on a home he is personally trying to sell, he may call you for his job before recommending you to his clients.

Restoring Old Houses

If you enjoy history, you might consider working on historic houses. Today, the demand for restoring historic homes has increased as people become aware of their value. Working on these homes can give you the satisfaction of preserving a part of the past and the enjoyment of learning about a specific area of history.

Before jumping into this specialty, know that there are certain requirements to working on historic homes. First, more times than not, the paint originally used on these homes had lead in it. Being "lead abatement certified" is necessary if you are considering working on older homes. Also be aware of asbestos and mold problems. Government standards for taking care of these health hazards exist as well. Second, when working on rehabilitating older houses, certain colors of paint and types of wallpaper need to be used. You will need to have enough historical savvy to know which colors were used in what time period or know where to learn about those details. A good place to start is the Historic House Colors website, www.historichousecolors.com. Here you will find information on color selection, links that can expand your knowledge, and a list of books and videos on the colors and design of historic homes.

To break into this specialized field, you have to be knowledgeable about what you are doing. Look at "The Secretary of the Interior's Standards for Rehabilitation" at www.nps.gov/history/hps/TPS/tax/rhb/stand.htm and contact your State Historic Preservation Office to learn of your state's requirements. To find the office in your state, visit www.nps.gov/nr/shpolist.htm.

To get this type of work, take the usual routes: word of mouth, advertising, talking to real estate agents, but also check into getting listed on the Preservation Directory, Historic Properties, and Old House Web websites (the URLs are in the appendix).

Apartments

Apartments can also be a lucrative source of work. When tenants move out, the apartment complex paints the apartments that will be put up for rent again. Sometimes apartment complexes have maintenance men who do this type of work, but more and more these maintenance men work on electrical or plumbing issues, leaving the paintwork to be contracted out. Periodically, apartment complexes will update their look by painting the exterior, common areas, and general offices. Getting in with one or two apartment managers may lead to more business as word spreads of your work.

Apartment work can be a mixed bag. You may be asked to paint empty apartments or you may be asked to paint a room or two in an apartment where a tenant is living. Remember to respect the people living next door. By keeping noise to a minimum, you will not disturb the tenants and will ingratiate yourself to the property manager.

To get this type of work, set up an appointment with the apartment complex's manager. Tell him what type of painting work you do—interiors, exteriors, fixing holes in walls, scratches in wood, ceilings, etc. Leave your card and periodically during the year mail him a flyer reminding him of the work you do.

Insurance Work

Another good avenue is restoration work after a fire or a flood. Once the insurance is paid, homeowners look for someone to paint their homes. You may have to submit a bid, but don't overlook this area. Typically a restoration job like this is like working on a new house. There is no furniture to remove and no carpet in the space to be painted. Because the homeowners have been displaced while the restoration work is being done, they will be eager to return to their home, so they will want the work done quickly.

The best way to break into this area is meet with homeowner insurance agents, tell them what kind of work you do, and leave business cards or brochures with them. Many times, after a disaster, they may call you and ask that you give them a paint bid for insurance purposes. Then, when the house is ready to be painted, they will call you back to do the job for the amount you quoted.

Moving Up the Ladder: From Amateur to Professional

Painting your own house and the houses of friends and relatives is a surefire way to gain experience, but now you have decided to go out into the real world and find money-paying jobs instead of working for a hot meal or cold drinks. You may not be able to charge the amount you would like to at the beginning, but the goal is to begin.

First, you need to decide if you want to work at this job part time or full time. Probably the best way to start is part time. Once you get enough jobs and make enough contacts to sustain your present salary, then you can move over to a full-time position. Starting and building a business takes time. Don't expect to go out and within the first month be making more than you are making at your present job. Business statistics tell us that we will hear ten noes for every yes. The key to this business as well as any other is persistence.

Once you begin, how do you learn more skills? How and where do you go to learn how to move from an amateur to a pro? Most of the older painters out there have learned by trial and error. There was no painter school when they started, and even today, those types of institutions are rare. However, there are ways to learn and to continue to expand your knowledge as you build your business. There are also ways you can learn the business early on.

On-the-Job Experience

Since there isn't exactly a "school" that teaches painting, most of what you learn will be on the job. You have probably been painting your own house for a few years, and that is how you decided to start this business. The more you paint, the more experience you will gain. You will learn what brush works for which job and whether a job should be rolled or sprayed. As time goes on, you will discover shortcuts and tips that work for you.

If you are hesitant to strike out on your own, you might want to work for someone else for a few years. Don't expect him to teach you everything he knows. He doesn't want the competition, but that shouldn't stop you from learning. Be observant. See how things should be done and how they shouldn't. Take the initiative to learn new skills and procedures, and take every opportunity to practice what you learn.

Another way to get some on-the-job training is to volunteer. Habitat for Humanity always needs workmanship when it builds houses. Besides being able to improve your skills, you will meet others in your line of work. Don't think volunteering is a waste of your time. You never know who you will meet or the contacts you will make. And these contacts can help you go far. Go to www.habitat.org to find where you can volunteer in your area.

Seminars, Conferences, Workshops

At different times of the year, in different parts of the country, you should be able to find seminars, conferences, or workshops to attend. The Painting and Decorating Contractors of America, www.pdca.org, hold an expo every year where you can learn about the newest products available, changes in paint, and any new government regulations instituted over the year. You can also make valuable contacts at the expo. See the appendix for more information about the expo.

Check with your local painters union. Sometimes it offers workshops and if it doesn't, it might be able to guide you to who does. Paint stores are also a source for workshops. Your local Sherwin-Williams store, www.sherwin-williams.com, may hold demonstrations on how to apply certain paint types.

By checking around you will find ample sources for meetings and workshops that can help you.

Self-Study

In today's digital age, there is no excuse not to be educated in the field you want to work in. For the painter, besides books about color and technique, there are DVDs like the Weekend Painter's Series, available at www.weekendpaintersdvd.com, and Internet clips that show you how to apply everything from stain to an exterior to wallpaper to an interior. You can go to www.youtube.com, search for house painting demonstrations, and watch a number of videos on painting techniques. Also be sure to check out the videos on www.house-painting-info.com.

The key is to learn all you can about everything you can in your particular field. Read, read, read everything in magazines and books. Go to the library, check out books on color. Learn about different types of woods, which wood will take stain the best, which wood is hard or soft, which surfaces can be painted, and which ones can't. Sign up for the paint stores' magazines. Besides presenting their products, they regularly include articles about some form of painting technique.

Buy, rent, or borrow teaching DVDs. If you want to learn pointers and techniques, many paint-related websites have DVDs you can purchase. If your interests lie in faux painting, there are many videos or DVDs that demonstrate techniques of specific kinds of faux walls. Check with your local library. Many have large selections of how-to DVDs.

Finding and Attending School

While there are no schools that will give you a "degree" in painting, there are places where you can further your knowledge base and expand your expertise.

The International Union of Painters and Allied Trades (IUPAT) has a school, the Finishing Trades Institute (www.finishingtradesinstitute.org). This school covers an overview of the construction trades, and you can earn credits toward a bachelor's degree in labor studies from the National Labor College (www.nlc.edu). Scholarships are also available through the union for those who qualify. Another place to find scholarships is through the American Federation of Labor and Congress of Industrial Organizations, more commonly known as the AFL-CIO (www.afl-cio.org).

The IUPAT offers apprenticeship programs as well, for those who want to earn money while learning a trade. Most programs last for three years. You will work with a mentor on real jobs getting paid with health insurance and benefits while becoming proficient in your field.

The only drawback to these offerings is that you or a parent must belong to the union to benefit. However, joining the union may be a plus for you if you feel you need a strong education background, so look into all the possibilities.

If you are looking to specialize in certain types of painting, check out faux painting. Parents-to-be and those wanting unique areas in their homes need someone who can take a blank wall and give it the *wow* factor. Expecting parents may want a mural or may have a specific theme in mind for the nursery, and other homeowners may want a wall to look like southwestern stucco or Grecian marble. Faux painting can offer you the ability to do just that type of work. Three of the biggest faux painting schools around are listed on page 16. While they may not offer a traditional degree, you will get hands-on experience in an area of painting that is lucrative and growing.

Prices for these classes, workshops, and degree programs vary from school to school. Besides the places mentioned earlier, check out your local home centers and

The **School of Applied Arts** (www.schoolofappliedarts.org) is in Denver, Colorado. This school focuses on decorative painting and offers a three-year degree in applied arts. Here you will learn wall-painting techniques like fresco painting, decorative plaster, wood graining, faux marble, mural painting, and portrait painting if your interests lie in that direction.

Martin Alan Hirsch runs the **Faux Finish School** (www.fauxfinish.com) in Louisville, Kentucky. The school opened in September 1992 and offers beginner and advanced painting classes and workshops. Unique in his approach, Hirsch makes sure that his students leave with not only knowledge about faux painting but about the business end of this career as well.

With two locations, one in Florida and one in Maryland, **The Faux School** (www .thefauxschool.com) holds one- to five-day workshops and classes on faux painting for residential and commercial structures. Ronald Layman, founder and director, has instructors who teach such classes as artistic concrete staining, Venetian and Italian plaster, marble and wood graining, plus other faux-painting techniques.

vocational schools. Periodically they will bring in guest instructors who are professionals in their fields to hold workshops.

Business Education

While knowing how to paint and what a painting business entails, it is just as important for you to be business savvy. Many businesses fail, not because the owner doesn't work hard, but because he doesn't use good business practices. Government rules and regulations change from year to year. You need to keep track of hourly wages, Social Security, and insurance, and that's just the beginning.

Junior colleges, vocational-technical schools, and business and trade schools offer small-business courses through their continuing education departments. These classes are usually held at nights or on weekends. Classes will vary but can include computer education, small business management, and bookkeeping skills, plus sessions on how to market and advertise your business. Some communities offer weekend workshops for the small business owner, and there are always many books available at bookstores or your local library to teach you how to run a small business.

Probably your greatest source for business information is the U.S. Small Business Administration, the federal agency that helps small business. Most of the time you will hear it referred to as the SBA. On the agency's website (www.sba.gov) alone, you can find data to download, forms, small business journals, information about small business loans and how to apply for and secure one, and more. The agency offers online training in business management, finance and accounting, getting government contracts, and surviving in today's slow economy.

If you need business counseling assistance and want to speak with someone face to face, the SBA has Small Business Development Centers across the United States. These centers assist small business owners with immediate counseling on financial matters, marketing, business organization, and several other business-related areas.

Another source of help through the SBA is the Women's Business Center. Through counseling and training, it offers to help women get started in business and to help their businesses grow.

The largest resource partner of the SBA is the Service Corps of Retired Executives (SCORE), which consists of more than thirteen thousand volunteers who have business skills in more than six hundred fields. These volunteers are either retired or working executives, business owners, or corporate businesspeople who share their knowledge and expertise with new business owners. In 2010, they gave 1.4 million hours of their time.

Each year, SCORE helps close to twenty thousand businesses get started. It holds local workshops, and offers face-to-face counseling and online training. Since 1964,

Face the Facts

There are companies out there that are successful and ones that aren't. Find one that is successful and model your company after it. Watch what it does. See what jobs it avoids and which it seeks.

SCORE has helped more than nine million people start their own businesses. To find a SCORE office near you, visit www.score.org.

As in all areas of business, there is a lot of information out there. You have to be willing to look for it, ask questions, and pursue any avenue that will help you improve and build your business. You will never be able to cover, know, or find all of the information available to you. It seems the more resources you look for, the more you find. Don't hesitate to ask for help. Asking for help does not make you look weak. It gives you the strength and knowledge to get your business on a solid foundation. If you don't find what you need in one place, go to another or ask for another place to look. Learn all you can about your business, yes, but don't neglect the business end of your business. That could be disastrous. You need to know how to paint, what kinds of paint to use on what surface, and the like, but you also need to know how to keep track of your money and how to spend it to get the most advantage for your business. You need to know how to find jobs and get jobs, and then who to hire to work with you. Throughout this book, you will find information on writing a business plan, finding employees, getting the word out about your business, legal issues, and more.

Running a business and learning about running a business never end. It isn't like a nine-to-five job. You need to continually learn about government regulations that may change in relation to your work, environmental issues regarding the products you use, and changes to tax and employment rules , to name just a few areas. Changes come and go like the wind. You need to know about all of those changes to help your business be successful.

02 Envisioning the Business

Let's start this chapter by getting you to think about what kind of business you want to own and operate. Are you looking to buy a business that already exists, or do you plan to start your business from scratch? Are you going to go at it by yourself, or do you have a partner you want to bring aboard? No matter which way you decide to go, you need to think about all of the ramifications that go with these decisions.

Buying an Established Business

When buying an established business, you need to look at several aspects of that business.

First, what kind of reputation does the business have? How does the current owner treat his clients? Is he true to his word? Can he be trusted? Has he taken care of problems with customers quickly? How has he treated his clients? How has he treated his business associates, contractors, and subcontractors? How has he treated his employees? Has he paid them on time? Has he let them slack off on the job? If the company you're buying doesn't have a good reputation, you will have a hard time finding work or perhaps keeping employees. Knowing what you have to work with from the start will help you decide whether you should purchase the business. Ask around. Other tradesmen will know if the current business owner is fair and has integrity.

Second, what type of work and how much work does the company have? You don't want to buy a business that is stagnant. If you have to start from the bottom, you can do that by yourself without the hassle of overhead like insurance, workers' compensation, and salaries if you have employees, and other expenses you may not have realized. Be sure to see the contracts the company has and then confirm those contracts. It's one thing for someone to say he has jobs; it's another thing for him to have secured the work.

Third, what shape is the equipment in? Check to see how new the equipment is, if it is still running, and when was it maintained last. Are all the parts available? If not, have the current business owner make a list of all missing parts. A good rule of thumb is to have the business owner list the equipment the company owns, when it was purchased, how much was paid for it, what attachments came with it (if any), and when it was last serviced. It would also be a good idea to have the owner give you a maintenance schedule for each piece of equipment. You don't want to buy a business and have to immediately start replacing all the equipment. That could turn into a lot of money fast.

Fourth, look at the books and have an independent auditor look at the books. You need to know how many liabilities the company has and how many assets. By getting an independent auditor to review the books, you will get an unbiased view of the company. You don't want to purchase a company that is deeply in debt.

Finally, check to see if the company has any liens or outstanding judgments against it. These could be a death knell to the company before you even get a chance to move in. Liens are a legal hold on a piece of property for which work was supposed to have been done or has been done. For instance, let's say a company bought paint from a paint store and painted a house, but didn't pay the paint store for the paint because the homeowners didn't pay the company. The paint store can put a "lien" on the property, which keeps the homeowners from selling their property until the lien is paid. If the paint company used a deficient paint or the wrong color and that is why the homeowners didn't pay, they may decide to sue the paint company because of the lien the paint store put on their house. In other words, if substandard work was done on their home, the homeowners typically feel that the paint company should rectify the work and pay the paint store for the expenses incurred in the mistake. If the homeowners decide to sue the paint company because of substandard work and the unfair lien they feel the paint store put on their property, this dispute could take a big financial bite out of your newly purchased business.

Starting from Scratch

If you are going to start from scratch, don't quit your current job. Think of what kind of work you have lined up. You will need to have at least three months of solid work before even considering making this job full time.

Are you actively talking to prospective clients who want or need their houses painted? Even when you get those three-month jobs, you need to keep actively looking for work. You don't just work a nine-to-five job anymore. Your work is full time.

Are you looking to stay small, as a one-man operation, or do you want to grow to a crew of ten or more? If you want to become big, you must plan for it in advance. There will be many decisions to face once people are working for you. We'll talk more about that later in the book.

What are your dreams or goals for this business? Write down a simple statement saying where you want this business to be in one year, five years, and ten years. This statement can become your mission statement. You must have a clear vision of what you want, in order to get where you want to go.

Going It Alone or with a Partner

When you run and own a business by yourself, you are the one solely making the decisions about what jobs you take, how the work is conducted, and where your money goes once the work is complete. With a partner, you will need to consult him on every aspect of the business.

Many years ago, my husband had two partners. They were happy to do the work, but all the administrative duties fell on my husband. He had to get the jobs, run the jobs, and afterward collect and do all the paperwork. His job was never ending. Since he worked on jobs as well, he decided one day that it wasn't worth all the time he was spending to work with partners when he could do what he was currently doing but without the hassles of those two partners. He disbanded the partnership, and his business has been less stressful ever since.

There are many considerations if you're thinking about going into business with a partner. Take the following short quiz to see if acquiring a partner would be helpful to you or more of a hindrance:

1. *Is your potential partner a friend?* The best way to end a friendship is to go into business together. It is one thing to see your friend every week or so. It's another to see him daily. The little tics that did not bother you before may become big problems. You have to see going into business with a partner like a marriage, because that is what it ends up being. Would you like to marry this person?

2. *How long have you known this person?* Most people wouldn't marry someone they met the day before. Use this same logic when taking a partner. A good

baseline is five years. In five years, you should know if the potential partner is a drifter moving from town to town or a fairly stable person who will stay in one location for more than just a few years.

3. *Is this person reliable, trustworthy, and hardworking?* Ask his friends and acquaintances if they have ever questioned his word. In your dealings have you ever had cause to question his integrity? Does he get up every day and go to work and get jobs done or does he play hooky and go fishing?

4. *What skills does this person bring to the table for your business?* If this person doesn't bring any skills to the business, why are you thinking about bringing him on as a partner? Is he good with numbers so he can help you with the accounting end of the business? Does he possess a skill you don't have, like being a good wood man? Maybe he can paint wood and has his technique down to an art? If you want to expand to more wood projects, he may be a good person to bring on board. If his skills won't enhance your business, there is no need for him to be a partner. The bottom line: A partner has to bring something that will benefit the business.

5. *What are this person's views on owning his own business?* Is he willing to put as much work into building the business as you are? You are excited and dedicated to building your company and making it a million-dollar business. If your partner wants to keep operations simple and small, you better look for another partner. Will he be willing to work late at night and on weekends to finish a job, or is he an eight-to-fiver?

6. *Is this person successful in his own right?* Has he been working on his own for quite a while, and does he continue to get work? Has he taken care of his family?

7. *Does this person have the same work ethic that you have?* When you send this person out on a job, will he do quality work? Will he give your clients the same respect and customer service you would give them?

8. *What kind of image does this person project?* Does he dress neatly? Is his hair neatly trimmed? You don't expect a painting partner to be a model, but he can't scare your clients either. If every other word out of his mouth is a cuss word, he might make some people uncomfortable. So think about how this person looks to others before you take him on as a partner.

9. *What kind of credit history does he have?* You need to check into a person's finances before you take him on as a partner. You don't want a partner with

a bad credit history because this may hinder you from getting loans you need in the future to expand your business. Second, if your partner is not careful with his own money, can you trust him to be careful with the business and not run it into the ground?

10. *What kind of personality does this person possess?* Is he laid-back and easygoing or a hothead who flies off the handle with each little problem? Your ideal partner should be someone who complements your personality. He should be motivated, but not to the point of making rash decisions, and laid-back, but not lazy.

After you have deliberated on all these questions, if you decide to take on a partner, find an attorney and draw up a partnership agreement. You will need to decide what percentage of the business each partner will own and state specifically what duties each will perform and who gets how much of the business should the partnership be dissolved. You must do this to protect your interests as well as those of your partner's. If your partner doesn't want to be part of a partnership agreement, you should think twice about going into partnership with him.

Before bringing on a partner, work with him on a few jobs to gauge his temperament. Decide if he is someone you can and want to work with. Partnerships can be great, but they can be a nightmare, too. On the plus side, a partner is someone you can share the financial burden with, someone you can bounce ideas and problems off of, and someone who can help you fix mistakes when they need to be fixed.

How Do You Want to Run Your Business?

When thinking of your business, you need to consider the legal and tax ramifications of each type of business. There are four business types—corporation, partnership, LLC, or sole proprietorship. Each has its pros and cons. Choosing one over another could make the difference between paying $1,000 or $10,000 a year in taxes. Let's take a look at each one and their advantages and disadvantages. As with all aspects of your business, sit down with an accountant and an attorney and discuss all your options to find out what is best for your business.

Sole Proprietorship

In a Sole Proprietorship, a single person owns and operates a company. According to the Internal Revenue Service, a sole proprietor is someone who owns an unincorporated business by himself or herself. It is the oldest, easiest, most inexpensive, and most common legal business to set up and maintain.

On the plus side, in this type of business, you are the boss, you have complete control over all that happens in the business, and you get all the profits. From a legal and tax standpoint, you and the business are one.

On the downside, you take all the risks. You will be responsible for checking with state and local authorities and securing any permits, business licenses, and registrations required. You are personally responsible for all taxes and debt. Because being a sole proprietor basically means you are self-employed, you won't be able to get workers' compensation or draw unemployment. Also, you are personally liable for any vendor fraud, lawsuits, or defaults on loans. So, if your business goes belly up financially, creditors can take your possessions, like your house, cars, paintings, etc.

For this type of business, you don't really have to do anything. If you don't incorporate, become an LLC, or enter into a partnership, your business will automatically be considered a sole proprietorship.

Two final considerations in a sole proprietorship: One, this type of business is easy to set up and dissolve. Two, when you die, the business dies.

Partnership

A *Partnership* is defined as when you and a partner—friend, relative, associate, or a group of partners—own a business together. Each partner brings his skills, expertise, and money to the business in return for a portion of the company's profits. Putting a partnership together is fairly simple. All you need is a partnership agreement. Make sure you get an attorney to write up and execute the partnership as you want to protect yourself and your partner(s).

When entering into a partnership, all partners are recognized as legal owners. Each partner has a say in the business and can hire or fire employees, borrow money, and maintain operations. Each partner is taxed on his share of the profits, and each is personally responsible for debts and taxes incurred by the business.

The pros of being in a partnership include having someone to bounce ideas off of, having someone who can bring something useful to the business through his skills, expertise, or contacts, and having someone to share expenses. A partner also is someone who has a share in the risks taken.

One con of having a partner is that each partner is legally responsible for what the other partner does in the business, so if you have a partner who is irresponsible with money or hiring employees, or who operates the business in a nonprofessional manner, that behavior is going to reflect on you. Another problem occurs when partners disagree on issues related to the company, such as when one partner thinks he should be making more than the other partner because he perceives himself to be putting more into the business. These situations can quickly turn ugly and destroy a business.

Limited Partnership

There is such an agreement as a *limited partnership*. In this type of partnership, there is typically a general partner who makes the decisions for the day-to-day operation of the business and a limited partner who has limited involvement in the business, but is a source of capital. The pros of this type of partnership are that you will have someone to bounce ideas off of and capital available if you need it. The cons are because you are the general partner if there are legal problems or the company fails, the general partner is fully liable while the limited partner is shielded from liability because he did not participate in the running of the business. Also, you will now have a partner who if you want to add another partner or change your role in the business, the general partner must get the limited partner's approval before you can move forward. This type of partnership must be registered with each state, and a franchise fee is required to file certification.

Once again, make sure you secure an attorney to help you set up all partnership agreements, regular or limited. Make sure you ask questions and get those questions answered before signing on the dotted line. The price you pay an attorney now and the questions you ask can potentially save you headaches and large amounts of money in the future.

Corporation

The Small Business Administration defines a *corporation* "as a legal entity separate from its owners, who own shares of stock in its company." Being a legal separate entity, a corporation has its own set of liabilities, rights, and privileges apart from its owners.

The downside of a corporation is that it is a complex and difficult business to set up. Corporations are held under stricter government regulations than any other type of business, have state filing fees when created, and have ongoing state filings and fees. A corporation has to hold annual board meetings, keep meeting minutes, issue stock certificates, and elect directors and officers like president, vice president, secretary, and treasurer. On the plus side, corporations project a good business image, have limited liability protection, and typically can raise capital more easily than other types of business.

There are two types of corporations, a C Corporation and a Subchapter S Corporation.

A C Corporation is a complex beast unto itself. It must hold to all the strict government regulations and licensing of a corporation, and is taxed double. This type of business is taxed at the corporate level and then again through stockholders' dividends.

The Subchapter S Corporation is like the C in many ways except in taxation. If a company qualifies for S status, the corporation is taxed like a partnership or a sole proprietorship. That means that the corporation is taxed at an individual rate rather than a corporate one.

Tips That Make Sense

If you want to save money and incorporate your business yourself, check out these three websites: My Corporation, www.mycorporation.com; Legal Zoom, www.legalzoom.com (click on Business Services); and BizFilings, www.bizfilings .com. These online companies allow you to do all your research, business filings, and reports on the Internet. While this is convenient, always check with an accountant or an attorney to confirm that your bases are covered.

You or your tax accountant can contact the Internal Revenue Service to see if you qualify for S Corporation status. You can also request IRS Pamphlet 589 to get an overview of S Corporation requirements.

LLC

A *Limited Liabilities Company,* also known as an LLC, is a fairly new legal designation of business. It is designed to allow "management flexibility" the way a general partnership does but provides the limited liability of a corporation. This means that you are taxed like a partnership but protected from personal liabilities like a corporation.

This type of business is recognized in all fifty states, although requirements and regulations may vary from state to state. Owners are known as members, and when forming an LLC, those members must file organizational articles with their state's secretary of state. Also at this time, each member must submit an operating agreement stating the relationship between him, the other members, and the company.

The pros of forming an LLC are that the paperwork of organizing and maintaining this type of business costs less than a corporation, you pay federal taxes as though you are in a partnership, and members have limited personal liability.

The cons are that this type of business costs more to set up than a sole proprietorship, the company dissolves when owner entity dies, and some states require that more than one person own and operate an LLC.

Tools and Equipment

For running your business, you will need the tools of your trade and office equipment. The tools you will need will vary from job to job, but there are standard tools you will use all the time. In the next section, we will go over the tools you will need in the field and at your office. As you buy tools and equipment, remember to purchase quality products. Most of your tools you will use every day. They need to be durable and able to stand up under all kinds of conditions. Like musicians, painters have favorite tools that they have used for years. My husband has used the same putty knife and brush for more than twenty years. They were more expensive than other products, but they have stood the test of time. He has purchased items on sale, and he has been sorry, as when the handle broke off a putty knife on its first use or when the bristles of a paintbrush start falling out on the fifth job. "There's nothing more frustrating than bristles getting stuck on the wall after you've cut it in," David says.

You don't have to buy all the items listed at once. Start out with one brush, one roller, one putty knife, and a drop cloth. As your business grows, you can gradually buy more tools and equipment.

Tools of the Trade

Tape Measure

Whether you buy or borrow a tape measure for your first job, you will eventually want to own a tape measure for your business. The average home typically has at least one, but if you are strapped for cash and don't own one, ask around. I'm sure you have a friend or a family member who owns one. You need a tape measure not only to provide a job estimate to your client, but also to figure out how many gallons of paint you will need for the job.

There are two types of tape measure on the market today—the standard and the laser. Both have their advantages and disadvantages.

The standard is the kind that has a physical metal tape you pull out. It is divided into one-sixteenth of an inch increments, so if you need to be precise with your measurements, you will need to learn how to read to the one-sixteenth. This type of measuring tape needs to be stretched across an entire room and locked in place, and then the measurements are read. The best way to use this type of tape measure is to have one person hold one end and another pull the tape. When the measurement is taken, you push or slide a button and the tape automatically retracts into its casing. The downside of the standard tape measure is having to wrestle with it yourself. Brands like Stanley and Lufkin are the most common and range in price from $5 to $15.

The second type is the laser measuring device. This device measures rooms with you standing on one side and pointing the laser to where you want to measure on the other side. Reports have stated that these are 99.5 percent accurate. Stanley has one that measures to one-fourth of an inch accurate to one hundred feet for $100. Zircon has a device that rounds to the nearest inch for $44, so if you are looking for averages, this is the instrument for you. The advantage is that you can do the measuring yourself without having to move around the room much. The disadvantage is that you will eventually have to replace batteries. But just keep a couple handy, and you will be fine.

Calculator

You don't need anything fancy here, just a small pocket calculator. Sometimes when you measure a room, the client wants an estimate right away. You can take your measurements out to your truck and do the figuring in minutes with a calculator. If it's a small job, you're better off to do it that way anyway. For larger jobs, I would wait, do the calculations back at the office, and e-mail or mail the estimates to your client. You can usually find small pocket calculators at your local discount store for a couple of dollars. If you have a dollar store in your area, you can typically find one for a buck.

Brushes

There are many types of brushes out there. You may be overwhelmed by the choices at the paint store, but we are going to narrow them down and tell you which brushes are the best for which jobs.

To start off, you really only need one brush—a nylon polyester. It works well for waterborne paints, which have become the standard for house paints because of the volatile organic compounds (VOC) in older paints. These paintbrushes are great for cutting in around windows and door casings and clean up well. A good general size is two-and-a-half inches, and Purdy is a good brand. A Purdy brush may cost a little more, around $15, but you want to get the best one your budget will allow because your brushes are your most used tools.

After you get one or two jobs under your belt, buy a few more brushes at different sizes. As you paint more, you will find that there are different kinds of spaces you need to get into. Different sizes of brushes will allow you to reach these areas.

If you are working on wood, purchase Purdy "syntox" brushes. These brushes have finer bristles than the nylon polyester, and they will help keep streaks to a minimum. Sizes are in half-inch increments, starting at one-half inch and running up to four-and-a-half inches. Purdy makes angle sash, which has a slanted edge and is good for cutting in, and flat tip, which has a straight edge. These brushes tend to be more expensive than other brushes but are well worth the price.

Also for wood, but for oil-based paint, are Purdy white china bristle brushes. These brushes also keep streaks to a minimum because their bristles are fine as well. Several sizes are available, and your choice of size depends on your need for the job.

Rollers

There are two types of rollers to consider. Paint rollers are three, six, or nine inches long. They are used to cover large areas of walls quickly.

When you are starting out, purchase a six-inch lamb's wool roller. The nap length on this roller is $3/8$ to $1\,1/4$ inches and gives a nice, smooth finish on flat walls and ceilings.

The other type of roller is synthetic. These rollers are typically cheaper than lamb's wool and come in the same length of nap. They are good to use for brick, block, or heavily textured walls because their fuzzy nap allows them to fill in cracks better than lamb's wool. An added bonus is that these rollers are considered throwaways. You can use them on one job and throw them out because they are so cheap.

Putty Knives

Putty knives are indispensable items you will use time and time again. They come in sizes ranging from $5/8$ inch to $1\,1/4$ inch. They are used for opening cans, patching small holes and cracks, and scraping off old paint. Hyde brand is the most durable and common. They range in price from $3 to $6 and can be found at your local paint store, Lowe's, or Home Depot.

Broad Knives

As your work progresses, you will want to invest in broad knives. Similar to putty knives, they range in size from one-and-a-half inches to twelve inches wide. These knives are used to fix dry wall and patch holes in walls. They can also be found at your local home improvement store.

Bucket Screens

These are useful to have because they help keep paint splatter and other messes to a minimum. They come in plastic or metal in three-, six-, or nine-inch sizes, to match roller sizes. The screen fits inside a paint bucket and allows a painter to get the paint evenly distributed on the roller. When paint is evenly spread out, it doesn't drip as much and is easier to apply to walls. A metal screen is recommended. They don't cost much more than plastic and will last you a lifetime.

Tape

You will want to keep an ample supply of taping supplies on hand. Through trial and error, painters have found two types of tape that are far superior to your basic tan masking variety. For masking around windows, you will want to use tape that releases easily. Because of the heat around windows, painters use products like 3M's Scotch Safe Release Tape, also known as Painter's Blue Tape. To mask off wood, the best product is 3M's 2060. This green tape seals well so as to not allow paint to bleed through to other surfaces and has a clean removal for easy peel off. Masking tapes range in price from $4 to $12. Don't be put off by the price. A quality product will allow you to do a quality job.

Sanding Pads

These pads have replaced the old sandpaper and for good reason. They are easier to grip and easier to use. They have a soft back and are made to do various jobs on various coatings. 3M has an entire line of sanding pads, and they vary in size and function. There are pads for waterborne paint, drywall, woodwork, and lacquer.

Around the Paint Bucket

On the Master Painters Institute (MPI) website, www.paintinfo.com, you will find the volatile organic compounds (VOCs) listed for paints, information on green products, and surface preparation for new paint products.

Each specific pad is made for a specific function. No more guessing about which grade to use.

Drop Cloths

From the beginning you will want to invest in some sort of drop cloth. Accidents and spills happen. You may step back and knock over a paint can or drop a brush or roller. You will want to have something to cover the area you're working in to keep messes and spills, and thus cleanup, to a minimum. Drop cloths vary in width from three to twenty feet. To start with, you may want to purchase the plastic ones. They are cheaper than the cloth ones and are considered disposable. Be forewarned, though, plastic drop cloths are slippery; they don't absorb paint, thus allowing for easy tracking of dropped or spilled paint through your work area.

Cloth drop cloths are a bit more expensive, but once the investment is made, they last a long time. Cloth ones are less likely to slip on the floor, and they absorb paint well. Make sure you purchase a drop cloth that is coated on one side, so paint won't seep through. Many a painter has had messes to clean up by not getting a coated drop cloth. My brother-in-law was almost sued when paint seeped through his drop cloth onto a carpet. Thank goodness, he only had to pay a professional carpet cleaner instead of buying new carpet.

Ladders

You may not need a ladder at the beginning of your painting career, but eventually you will need to make the investment. A painter typically has three or four on his truck. Stepladders range from two to sixteen feet (tall enough to reach a high ceiling).

A step up is the extension ladder. These typically range from eight to forty feet tall and allow you to reach even higher ceilings and do most outside work on houses. Anything higher, you will need to work on scaffolding or lifts and tie off by securing yourself to the scaffolding or lifts with ropes or belts. Typically there are places to tie off to on this equipment. Scaffolding can be purchased at the same place as ladders, but that is something to think about down the road.

When buying a ladder, think about safety. Ladders come in types 1, 2, and 3. You will want to purchase a type 3 if your budget allows. These are sturdier ladders and will last longer. Also, it is important to look for ladders made of fiberglass, because you are often working around electricity. There have been too many reports of painters being electrocuted because they come in contact with electricity while standing on a metal ladder. Fiberglass is just as strong as metal, so think safety first.

Ladders average about $10 a foot, so a six-foot ladder will cost around $60. If your budget won't allow you to purchase your own ladders right away, see about borrowing them from friends or relatives or renting them by the day from your local home improvement store.

Airless Sprayers

As you pick up more work, you may want to consider purchasing an airless sprayer. An airless is used for painting large areas, exteriors, and ceilings quickly. It uses hydraulic pressure to force paint at about three-quarters of a gallon per minute through a hose out of a gun onto a surface. Three thousand pounds of pressure comes out of the tip of the gun, so it is a serious piece of equipment. Typically the paint store will give demonstrations on how to use one.

Prices range from $400 to $5,000, and most come with about fifty feet of line or air hose. Graco brands are solid and durable, and most come with a one-year warranty. If the price is out of your range, consider renting an airless or ask about purchasing a demo. You can typically get a demo for half the price of a new one.

While the gun that comes with the airless is vital, the most important part of the gun is the tip. You have to use the right size tip for the paint product used. For instance, the smaller the tip, the finer the product has to be. Tips range from 2/12 to 12/35. The first number is the width the tip will spray in inches. The second number is the orifice size, which is how big the tip is.

Respirators and Masks

For sanding or working in poorly ventilated areas, consider purchasing respirators and masks. This protective gear filters out harmful particles and fumes. Two kinds are available. One is a paper throwaway mask that fits over your nose and mouth much like what surgeons use. The other kind is a respirator. These are masks as well, but they have filters that keep out even more harmful materials floating in the air. Both can be found at home improvement stores, or you can order them online from Uline or 3M.

Cleanup Material

The best all-around cleaner is trisodium phosphate, better known as TSP. It can be used before you paint to remove dirt, grease, and mildew on inside and outside surfaces. Be sure to mask off areas you don't want affected by TSP. It will turn surfaces white or leave a film. After work, use it to clean brushes, paint screens, and buckets. Wear gloves when using the product as it can cause skin irritation and even burns. TSP comes in one- to four-pound containers and can be found at home improvement stores.

Around the Paint Bucket

Wol-Wax (pronounced "wool" wax) is a great cleaner, polisher, and thirst quencher for wood. When my brother-in-law finished up the wood in our house, he handed me a twelve-ounce bottle of Wol-Wax and told me to clean the wood with it. The first time I used the product, I was sold. More than twenty years later, the wood in my house looks brand new. We typically buy a gallon and give it to people for their newly finished wood. It comes in concentrate, so a little will go a long way. A twelve-ounce bottle will typically last me three years, and I have a *lot* of wood.

Faux Painting Supplies

The following is a list of some items you will need if you decide to become a faux painter. Of course, there are other items beyond what is listed here, but this will give you a good start.

Sponges

Sponges are a great tool to have when faux-painting walls. Round, square, big, and small, they can help you cover areas faster and easier. Marine sponges of all shapes, sizes, and types are good too, as they will help you introduce new effects on your walls like clouds, bushes, and grasses.

Specialty Brushes

Brushes are a good investment to make to help with details. Decorator's brushes in various sizes, fan, flat, filbert, liner, scroll, and round brushes all will assist you as you work on accent walls. Don't skimp on cheap brushes here. As stated before, cheap brushes will lose their bristles. You will probably catch your breath as you get ready to shell out $12 to $18 a brush, but with a good investment and proper care, these brushes will last a lifetime. Most of these you will find in a hobby, craft, or art store.

What to Wear on the Job

Over the years there has been a lot of discussion about what painters wear on the job. Most painters wear white. There are many reasons, starting with the legend of a king who wanted his virgin women's temple painted white. He told his painters to wear white so they would look pure when they entered the temple. Now, whether that story is true or not, there are other, more practical reasons painters wear white.

When paint started being applied on houses, white and red were the two most common colors used because they were the cheapest. People painted their houses white and barns red. Today, 90 percent of all colors painters use is white, so if painters do get paint on them they can still look neat and clean. White distinguishes the house painter from other tradesmen, and history tells us that union painters started wearing whites in the early twentieth century to separate themselves from nonunion painters.

Another consideration is that in summer when painters work outside, white reflects the heat and thus keeps them cool. Jackie, a painter's wife, says "whites" are easier to keep clean. Just throw them in hot water with some bleach. If painters are using different colors, whites also allow them to see the paint, keeping them from getting it on areas where they don't want paint, like expensive furniture.

According to Allen, a painter for fifteen years, you can tell a good painter by what his "whites" look like. If they are covered in paint and not clean, then he is a bum, but if they are crisp and clean, then he's worth more than the bristles on his brush.

A pro painter doesn't get paint on his "whites." They are great at what they do. They are fast and very neat.

My husband has always worn whites, and so has his crew. That's their uniform. Whites come in shirts and pants or overalls. Every painter has his preference. Whites can be found at many paint stores. Most painters buy their white pants there and then add white cotton T-shirts to complete their look. The cost ranges from $15 for pants to $45 for a pair of overalls.

Miscellaneous Extras

For regular and faux painting, a few extra items you might want to keep on hand are one or two trowels, a mud pan, a caulk gun, rags, and paper towels. Trowels are used to move plaster or mud around on walls when you are texturing or patching a large hole or crack with drywall. Pool trowels tend to be more popular as they have rounded corners instead of straight ones and move material around easier. They are metal and range in price from $4 to $20 depending on the size, which can be two to twelve inches.

A mud pan is a metal tray-type tool that will hold your drywall or patch material. A mud pan can be easily held in your hand, and with the way the sides are built, it makes loading and cleaning blades easy. One good metal mud pan will last a lifetime. They range in price from $10 to $30.

When filling cracks and small holes, you will most certainly have to caulk. To get the caulk to come out of the tube, you will need a caulk gun. You can find these at any hardware or home improvement store. They cost around $8 and should last a lifetime. David has had one for twenty years, and it's still going strong.

On every job you will need rags and paper towels. Buying rags can be expensive as they can cost around $20 a box. A cheaper solution would be to ask relatives and friends to save old bath towels, dish towels, sheets, T-shirts, and cloth diapers for

Around the Paint Bucket

To keep from messing up a wall and possibly your paint job, wrap the ends of your ladders with rags. This will keep them from marring the walls.

you. You can also go to secondhand stores and see what they have available. Designate a bucket or box to hold your rags. There's no need to buy anything new because you want the lint out of anything you use anyway. Lint getting on your walls is as bad as paintbrush bristles. Don't buy the most expensive paper towels. The cheap brand will work for your purposes. They will mainly be used to clean up floor messes and to rest your brushes on while drying after cleanup.

Finally, your most important piece of equipment will be your wheels—a truck or van. Painters are known to use either. David uses both. These vehicles will take you to and from jobs, carry your equipment, and in some cases become your office. You need not buy a new vehicle at first. A used one will probably make you feel more comfortable. Keep in mind that these vehicles need to transport all of your equipment, including ladders, airless sprayers, and your supplies, paint, tape, etc. If you have a used vehicle, you won't feel quite so bad if there is a spill in the back or if something leaks and gets on the floor.

Storing Your Stuff

Once you have all of your equipment and supplies, where do you keep them at night? At the beginning, you might keep them in your truck or van. If you have ladders, it would be wise to chain them to your vehicle as these items have been known to walk off.

As your business grows and you get more equipment, store it in your garage or get a storage shed. If you live in an apartment, rent a small storage unit. The key to storage is security. Lock your vehicle and lock the place in which you store your equipment. Many a painter has left to go to work only to find his equipment gone. If you leave your equipment on the job site, make sure it is secure as well. You can also purchase big lockboxes to put your equipment in. These are freestanding so make sure they are in a location where someone can't back up and drive off with them.

Keep Equipment Clean

A word here needs to be added about keeping your tools clean and properly maintained. A good habit to get into is to clean your tools every day as you finish your work. Since most paints today are waterborne, most of your tools will clean up with soap and water. Keep an empty paint bucket with a lid in case you are in too big of a hurry to clean up immediately. You can put your brushes and rollers inside the bucket, close the lid, and they won't dry out, making cleanup easier when you do get around to it. If the job is new construction, take a water hose to the job with you and clean your tools there. If it's an existing home, wait until you get home.

Cleaning an airless sprayer is a bit more time-consuming, but well worth it when you consider the time you will save from dealing with lines and guns getting stopped up. Since the airless is your biggest expense and will cost you a good chunk of change to get fixed, it would behoove you to learn all you can about the machine, so if something does go wrong you can fix it yourself. The problem may be simple enough to fix yourself, but if you don't know anything about the airless, you could lose up to a day's work by having to take it in. So learn to troubleshoot. It can save you time, which means saving you money.

03

Getting Started

So now that you know what kind of business model you want to follow and have an idea about the equipment you will need, let's cover setting up your home office, opening up bank accounts, and obtaining insurance, so you can get to work.

Working from Home

We started out with having an office from home, then moved into an office building for a year, and then went back to a home office. A home office was more convenient. David was typically on the job site with his crew, and while we had small children, it was more convenient to do all the work from home.

Now after all these years, we find the home office is more convenient and more economical for us. I am there during the day, available to answer phones, get faxes, or send blueprints by Fed-Ex, and then after David gets off the job, he bids blueprints, works out schedules, and communicates with his contractors. Through the years we have found what does and does not work in a home office.

First, when thinking about a home office, check with your city or county officials to see if there are any regulations, restrictions, or fees to having a home office. Most municipalities and counties won't mind as long as you aren't running a store from your home and people aren't coming and going, but it's best to make sure. You don't want to get up and running and then be fined and/or kicked out of your own home. If you are renting your home or apartment, check with your property manager. Besides getting information about rules and restrictions, you may pick up work after he knows what you are doing.

Second, designate a specific area to be your office. The Internal Revenue Service is very picky about this sort of deduction. You need to have one area where you do your work. Get a desk, a file cabinet, a phone, and any other office equipment you might need.

Third, when you can afford it, get a business telephone line and some way to receive faxes. A business line will help you separate personal calls from business, which will please the IRS, and your family should know not to answer the business line. If you are working the business by yourself, you might want to invest in an answering machine. You can leave a message to people who call, asking them to leave a message or call your cell phone. At first, you might want to consider using your cell phone strictly as your business phone. We did that for years, and it worked for us.

Eventually you will want to have some way to send and receive faxes. For years, we had a fax machine hooked to a land line, but when David started traveling, he needed a way to get architectural changes, paint notices, insurance certificates, etc., so we changed our home office fax to MyFax, (www.myfax.com) an Internet-based fax. We still have the same fax number, but he receives all of his faxes online through his e-mail. It is more convenient for him, and he has them when he logs into his e-mail wherever he is.

Fourth, set boundaries early on. If you have small children, set rules that they need to be quiet and play away from the office area when their parents are on the phone. They shouldn't be allowed to disturb any papers or equipment in the office, and you should be off-limits for certain periods of time. This isn't to ignore or be mean to your children, but you can get work done more quickly if you are undisturbed. You might explain that to your children as a way to make them understand the importance of this time.

Decide what your office hours are and stick to them. Sometimes working from home can be an all-consuming project. Determine that these are the hours when the office is open, these are the days you're working, and these are the days off. When you are off, close the door and leave it alone. You may hear the phone ring, but resist the urge to answer it. You have hours, stick to them.

When friends find out you have an office in your home, they may believe they can drop by anytime, unannounced, to shoot the breeze. Be firm by telling them that you're working or put a DO NOT DISTURB sign outside your door. Family members may consider your working at home as not really working and call, wanting you to do things for them. Do not fall into the trap of agreeing. Tell them that you are working and that maybe you can help on your next day.

Finally, when you are in your home office, you need to be disciplined. Your goal is to work, not to call friends or play games on your computer. Get your mind set early, and you won't have any trouble working in your office at home.

Setting Up Your Office

Office on Wheels

Before we begin talking about setting up your home office, I'd like to address your rolling office or the office in your truck or van. Because a lot of your business will be done out of your truck, you need a way to keep track of all of your business receipts, invoices, schedules, and more. In the beginning, you may choose to use a shoebox or a plastic box to hold all your receipts and separate them later, but once your business starts growing, you will probably want to use something a little more sophisticated.

First, you need to get a plastic file box. They range in price from $5 when on sale to $20 when not. This filing box will become your best friend, as it will be a general location for all your information. Next, invest in a hanging folder for the box and a package of pocket file folders.

Make separate files for your proposal or bid sheets, invoices, and each of the twelve months—January, February, March, and so on. In the proposal or bid sheet file, keep your proposals so if a client needs a bid right away, you can go out to your truck and write it up immediately. Invoices are needed in your truck because when you finish a job, you can write up an invoice right then. Who knows, you might get paid immediately as well. In the month folders, you can drop receipts for gas, food, paint, and any other items related to any given job. You can also keep your proposals and invoices in the months that you gave them.

A few extra items to keep in your truck are a clipboard to use when filling out your proposals and invoices, a tape measure, a calculator, your business cards, and several pens.

If you watch for sales, you can purchase all of the items for your truck office for around $50. These items will be worth the price once you get started and you need them.

Your Home Office

There are going to be times when you will need to work in your home office. Since you have designated one area of your home, conceivably a room separate from the living room, let's see if it will meet your needs. Is it private? Can you make calls without sounding as if you are in a tavern or at a ball game? Is it a room where you can close the door so you won't be disturbed? Will your work items be secure? Will a desk, chair, and file cabinet fit in the room? Do you have access to a phone line?

If you have answered yes to those questions, you've found the right room.

Furniture and Accessories

A desk is a necessity to any office. It doesn't have to be fancy, but it does have to have a flat writing surface. You can use a card table to start off with or build your own desk. When we first started in the business, we used two two-drawer file cabinets positioned on each end and laid a wooden door across the tops of the cabinets for the desktop. We did eventually graduate to a store-bought desk, but the file cabinet desk served our purposes for many years. You can make this kind of desk for less than $100.

Second, you need to give consideration to an office chair. To start with a folding metal chair will be just fine as long as you are limiting your time in the office. As you begin to spend more time in front of your computer, you may want to invest in a comfortable "office" chair. Every chair fits everybody differently. When you're ready to buy a chair, my suggestion would be to look at what fits into your price range and then sit in all of those chairs to find the one that is comfortable for you. Think of your chair as an investment not only for your career but also for your body.

Third, you need file cabinets. In your file cabinets keep a file for each job. Keep a copy of your proposal; quotes on paint from paint stores; any special modifications you had to make; personal notes such as if you had trouble with the homeowner or if the occupants of a home have allergies; invoices; and if you were paid in a timely manner.

Small items like a clock, a calculator, pens and pencils, a stapler, a calendar, in and out stack files, and a letter opener can be picked up here and there, when you have the money. A clock to hang on the wall is the best choice. Hang it in front of you, so you can look up at a glance and see the time. A desk calculator in the office is a better choice than a small pocket calculator. A printed tape will help you with calculations before, during, and after jobs.

Phone

You will need a phone. This is essential because it will be the tool you use to stay in touch with your clients, and located in this room, it will allow you the privacy you need to conduct business. A separate business line is a good idea if you have adolescents or young people in your house. It doesn't sound professional if someone else in the house picks up the phone while you're talking on the line. If you can't afford a separate line, an alternative is to get a phone system that alerts the rest of the household when you are on the phone. There are systems that read "line in use" and others that flash when someone is using the phone in another part of the house.

Computer

Next, let's talk computers and the accessories that go with them.

Computers are a big part of any business these days. They store data and allow you to recover that data easily and quickly. Since you will probably be doing everything for your business yourself, especially in the beginning, a computer is a good investment. For example, if you want to run an ad in your local paper, you can now design it or write it up yourself, zap it to the paper via e-mail, wait for the paper to send you proofs, and then send the paper payment via check or credit card. No more driving down to the paper, waiting to meet with someone, and coming back to view the proofs before the ad is printed.

The downside of owning a computer, and what I have seen as the reason for most resistance, is the time it takes to learn how to operate one. If turning on and pushing buttons terrify you, take a computer class at your local vocational-technical school or find a young person to teach you. The younger generation is fearless when it comes to anything electronic. In no time, they will have you up to speed in all things "computereez."

Once you figure out the ins and outs of a computer, you'll appreciate the time and energy you spent learning to use it. The following are some areas in which a computer can assist you as you build your business:

- *Bidding Jobs:* When working on a bid for a paint job, it is more efficient to put it together on a computer. You can make a template to use for each job, plug in your information and numbers like square feet, paint cost, etc., and then look at the bottom line. See bid information in chapter 5 to learn how to bid a job. Before you print it out and give it to the customer, it is easy to adjust because all you have to do is change numbers if needed.

- *Blueprints:* In this electronic age looking at blueprints on the computer is standard. Gone are the days when you would pick up a set of blueprints. Now, they are sent via e-mail in a zip file. If you decide to turn in bids on new houses or apartments, this is how you will be looking at the square footage and getting your calculations.

- *Job Record Keeping:* After putting together that bid, you can make a computer file for that job and save all the information together. For instance, let's pretend you have a client named Smith. In the Smith computer file, you can put the bid, paint specs, any correspondence with the client, any notes you might want to keep on the job, and the invoice. When you need to check what has been done on the job, you simply open the file and all the information will be there for you to peruse.

- *Bookkeeping and Tax Records:* A computer will allow you to keep track of your expenses and profits easily. From your computer, you can build a spreadsheet using Excel, a Microsoft program. This will allow you to separate and chart expenses like gas, food, paint, insurance, and other items. You will also be able to plug in how much you are paid from each job. After you subtract your expenses from your revenue, you will see how much you really made on certain jobs.

  By using a computer and spreadsheet at the end of the year, you can add up all of your expenses in categories. This will make doing your taxes easier as you will have all your information in front of you and compartmentalized.

  You can also make a spreadsheet for those who have paid you for jobs and those who need to pay you.

- *Communications:* Probably the best way a computer can help you is by allowing you to communicate with your customers through the Internet and e-mail. If there are quick questions that need answering, after-hours discussions that need to be taken care of, or you are just running late and need to remind a client or vendor about something, e-mail is always available to you no matter what time of day or night.

- *Research:* If you haven't been on the Internet much, you will be amazed at the amount of information available to you. You can look up government regulations regarding job safety, VOCs of paint products, and historical paint colors if you are doing restoration work on old houses. If you can't find it online, you will most certainly find out where you can go get the information in the real world.

- *Building a Database:* A database with information on your clients, contacts, and vendors will make a big difference in how efficiently you communicate with them. A list of your clients, their addresses, phone numbers, and e-mail addresses will make contacting them a breeze. Once you have a database, you can send out postcards, keeping your name in front of them, or send brochures announcing any specials you may have at the time. With a database, you can separate private home clients from home builders, insurance agents, and real estate contacts. Let's say you've added some special skill to your painting repertoire. It's a specialty your upper-class painting clients would be interested in instead of your new home builders. So you can go into your database, separate the names, and send postcards announcing your new skill to those clients you think may be interested.

  Keeping track of your vendors will help you if you need to contact several paint companies at once to find the price of a certain type of paint. Sort out the paint companies, grab their e-mail addresses, and send them your questions. Contacting five or six people all at once beats calling them one at a time.

- *Advertising:* There are so many things you can do regarding advertising on a computer that it's a wonder how anything was done even ten years ago. Now, you can build a website and have your storefront open all the time. This is an easy way to get people familiar with your business, what you do, how much you charge, and how to contact you. Consider your website to be your continual brochure.

  If you want to print flyers or brochures, that's easy to do with a computer too. There are many sites that have templates you can download for flyers and brochures. All you do once they are downloaded is fill in the spaces. You can also design your advertising material and then e-mail it to a printer or newspaper.

  We'll cover more information about promotional material, including websites, in a later chapter.

What Type of Computer Will You Need?

Now that we've talked about what a computer can do for you, let's talk about specific computers and which would be best for you. For all of the innovations in the computer world, we are still looking at two types of systems when it comes to computers, Windows-based personal computers and Macintosh from Apple. Both are okay, however, you have to be aware of the programs and systems that will be compatible with the type of business applications you need. Study both before you buy, and ask questions if you're not sure.

We've only used Window-based systems and have found that they do everything for us we have ever wanted them to do.

Once you decide which system you want, you need to decide if you want a desktop or a laptop computer. Currently, we have both. If you can only afford one, however, we would recommend a laptop. First and foremost, they are portable. You can take them in your vehicle and then bring them in at night to use at your desk.

No matter which one you choose, desktop or laptop, consider its functionality. You will need to make sure your computer can connect to the Internet, is fast, and has storage space. With that said, when buying a computer, buy a data storage system too. These range in physical size from the size of a paperback to a small penknife that will fit on your keychain. In storage capacity, you can get 2 gigabytes all the way up to 500 gigabytes. Whatever you do on your computer, you need to back up your information on some sort of storage device. There are two online data storage systems that can back up your information immediately—Mozy (www.mozy.com) and Carbonite (www.carbonite.com). You get a certain amount of free storage, and then you can pay a monthly fee for unlimited storage. I like these two systems because if your computer crashes, you can access your information from any other computer as long as you have your access code.

As far as the cost of a computer, that ranges. Sometimes you can get a computer for a few hundred dollars. If you watch for sales, you can find a good computer pretty cheap. Technology is changing all the time, and so are prices. Check around, and you will find a good deal. Look into refurbished or used systems. You can pick these up for pennies on the dollar of new computers.

If you choose a desktop computer, you will have to consider a monitor to go with it. Your eyesight and your office space should determine the size of your monitor. A seventeen-inch monitor is a good size to consider, and go with a flat screen, as it takes up less space. If you pick a laptop but would like a larger screen in your home office, buy a larger monitor and hook it up to your computer when you get home. That way you have the best of both worlds. Flat-screen monitors can run from $75 to $300, sometimes less if you catch a sale.

Check Out All Your Options

An option to go with a laptop would be to purchase a "smart phone." They are much smaller than laptops, and you can do almost as much with them as a computer. Smart phones come with a keypad or touch screen technology. The more popular smart phones are the Blackberry and the iPhone. Through different applications (more commonly called "apps"), these phones allow you to have an address book, organizer, and calendar; write memos and e-mail; access documents and files; and keep an eye on the news, weather, or other websites. One smart phone dealer boasts that it has more than thirty thousand apps. The great news is you can sync or send the material on your smart phone right over to your computer. These phones can be found at your local electronic or specialty electronic store and range in price from $99 to $600. The price usually depends on which service plan you choose and whether you are upgrading or buying the phone outright. Make a list of questions before you look at phones. Think about what you want your phone to do for you, what coverage you need, and how much business you want to conduct on it. Thinking about this beforehand will help you when you get to the store. You will get exactly what you want and need.

Software and Accessories

Some computers come loaded with certain kinds of software. While you may want to play around with what's available to you at the time, eventually you will want to upgrade. A good accounting program will help you at tax time plus make paying bills and doing payroll a breeze. I like Quicken or Quickbooks because they are dedicated to bookkeeping and have a lot of bells and whistles in their programs. You will also need a good general software package that includes a word processing program, a spreadsheet and database program, and an e-mail organizer, which should include a calendar and to-do list. Microsoft Office covers all those bases. These software programs will get you far in your business; from there you might want to look at business-specific software. There are a few programs for the house painter, but they come and go, so do a search and find out the latest software innovations that fit you and your business.

Other equipment you need to consider are a printer, scanner, copier, and fax machine. I listed all four because the biggest bang for your buck will probably be to buy an all-in-one machine. The advantages of an all-in-one are that it is easier to set up, takes up much less space, and is simpler and convenient to use once you learn the nuances and operations of the machine. An all-in-one is much cheaper to buy than four separate machines, but will still run $150 to $400.

The disadvantage to an all-in-one is that, if one part breaks down and you have to get it fixed, all four of your machines are gone while it is in the shop.

Backup and Internet Connection

Once you get your computer and its accessories, you need to think about two other items. First, you need to get a backup battery power supply or "UPS," uninterrupted power supply. What the backup power supply does is, if the electricity goes off, it allows you time to save your information before your computer starts shutting down. Also most come with a surge protector, which you will need if you live in an area that has a lot of lightning. If your computer ever gets fried once, you will appreciate the money spent to spare that from happening again.

If you are on a laptop during the day, you will be running off the battery. Make sure your laptop has long battery life. There are those available with nine-hour battery life.

Second, you will need to consider how you want to communicate with the outside world on your computer—broadband, satellite, DSL (digital subscriber line), or cable modem. While all are acceptable, if financially possible get broadband or satellite. We have found those more reliable and faster. Go with what you can afford, but definitely try to stay away from dial-up. Dial-up is slow, and you may turn gray-headed before you complete your first search.

Office Supplies

To finish your office, you need to consider a few more small supplies: paper, envelopes, stamps, tape, a stapler with staples, scissors, a letter opener, paper clips, file folders, colored markers, and pre-inked stamps. Paper and envelopes will be used not only for correspondence, but to print off bids and invoices and to mail them. You can staple receipts together from certain jobs and use the file folders for keeping information on your jobs. Purchase pre-inked stamps that say "file," "done," "send," "complete," "original," "paid," and "copy." It may sound like a lot of trouble, but you need to keep a hard copy of all your bids and invoices. You can't remember everything and if someone tries to cheat you, you will have the written proof about what was agreed upon.

These items may seem trivial until you need them. Then you'll wish you had bitten the bullet and purchased them. They don't cost that much, and many times you can find all these items on sale. The best time to shop for them is when the office supply stores have school supplies on sale or at the end of the year when stores are having sales getting ready for inventory.

Bank Account

From the start you will need to open a business account separate from your personal account. This will make your life a lot easier come the end of the year and at tax time. What kind of documentation you need to take to the bank will depend on how you have set up your business: sole proprietorship, corporation, LLC, or partnership. Call your bank to find out what you need to bring to open an account.

A word about your bank and banking account: I would choose a bank you have been personally doing business with for a number of years. In today's Internet age, this will allow you to transfer money electronically from your business account to your personal account, thus saving on writing checks to yourself. Second, be forewarned, when you start doing business and you deposit large checks, $5,000 and over, banks put a hold on your account until the check clears. Sometimes they will go ahead and clear the check so you can use it. Don't count on it, but you can always ask. We will talk about getting to know your bank president in chapter 6.

You can open a savings account at the same time or wait until you are paid from your first job. But plan on opening that account. Throughout the year, you will have expenses: One of the largest will be the cut Uncle Sam wants. By opening a savings account, you can move a percentage of what you make into that account, so you will have money for insurance and to pay your taxes. You should plan for 33.3 percent going to taxes and 10 percent to cover insurance. If you make saving this money a priority when you first start, you will be ahead in the long run.

Time to Talk Insurance

This may be every businessman's least favorite topic, but if you own or run your own business, it is something you need to seriously consider and address. In today's "sue first, ask questions later" society, it is best to consider options before problems occur.

At times, it seems that all insurance is good for is to take your money . . . until you need it. Then the insurance is well worth its price. Accidents will happen. You will get sick. Work will slow down. It is best to have all the bases covered, so you can do what you do best, and that isn't worrying about insurance.

You will want to find a reputable company and a dependable insurance agent who can help you set up all your insurance or at least can direct you to where to get certain types of insurance. You don't want to use an insurance company that may close its doors in a year after you have paid premiums. And you also want an agent who will be straight with you, not undersell but not oversell either. Check with the Better Business Bureau and other businesses, and don't be afraid to ask hard questions of your agent. If your agent can't or won't answer your questions to your satisfaction, find another. Also, be aware of your state's requirements and restrictions regarding insurance. Most states have websites that offer information on their insurance regulations and their statutes and rules related to insurance codes, like the Oklahoma Insurance Department's site. If you don't have a clue about finding an agent, contact the Independent Insurance Agents and Brokers of America. You can visit its website at www.iiaba.net or call (703) 683-4422.

If you are working by yourself, there are some insurance types you may not need, for instance workers' compensation, but we will discuss all types of insurance here so you will know what they are and how much they will cost you.

The following are different types of insurance you *need* to consider for your business:

- *General Liability:* This type of insurance, in simple terms, covers injury or property damage caused by you to others while you are on the job. For instance, if you spilled five gallons of paint on a $10,000 area rug, your general liability would pay to replace the rug. If you were painting on a ladder outside and slipped and fell through a window and broke it, your general liability would pay to replace the window and any other damages incurred as a result of the accident.

  Besides health insurance, this is probably one of the most important insurances you can have. If you don't have it and you damage someone else's property or they "think" you damaged their property, you may not only be out thousands of dollars, but you may be financially ruined if you have to come up with the money yourself. There are exclusions and limits on every general liability policy, so check those and discuss any concerns you have with your agent. Prices vary. You don't have to get the most expensive, but you shouldn't get the cheapest either.

- *Commercial Property Insurance* provides coverage for physical items like equipment and tools that you own. You may think you don't own enough to need coverage, but lose all of your work equipment in one robbery, with no money to replace it, and your business will be in big trouble real fast.

  Don't assume your homeowner's policy will automatically cover your business equipment. Most homeowner's policies don't. Some insurance companies offer special riders on their policies that can include business property insurance, but you need to ask for it and expect premiums to be upward of $200 a year.

  There is a business owner's policy you can purchase if you own thousands of dollars of equipment and a separate storage shed for it. Know up front that these policies are expensive. Home business insurance is another option. It is less expensive than a business owner's policy, but there are exclusions, so investigate and ask questions before you give a deposit.

- *Vehicle Insurance:* There are many ways you can go when obtaining insurance for your work vehicle. If it is old, you may not want to have body coverage on it. Liability insurance is required in all states, and you can typically choose the amount you want to be insured at. Liability covers you for bodily injury or damage to another's property in a car accident.

  If your vehicle is fairly new and you carry expensive equipment in it, you might want to consider comprehensive coverage that would be included in a full coverage policy. This would allow you to claim and recover items if they were stolen from inside your car. Most people think that their homeowner's or renter's policy will pay for items stolen from their car, but they don't. Each policy is different. Check yours out before assuming you are covered.

  If your employees will be driving your car, ask about adding them when you get your policy. This will continue coverage in case they are in an accident while in your vehicle. If they have good driving records, it should only cost you pennies on the dollar to add them.

- *Business Interruption Policies:* You might want to consider this type of insurance after your company gets going and grows a bit. These policies help you against a loss in profits and cover your expenses should you suffer a loss of property, if, for example, a fire destroys your business and equipment. Check out an overhead policy as well. If loss or illness occurs, this type of policy will cover insurance premiums, workers' salaries, rent, utilities, and interest payments until your business is able to recover. These policies are not cheap, so think long and hard before investing in them.

- *Health Insurance:* Insurance has become part of the American landscape. With today's laws making health insurance a requirement, not much needs to be said about this type of insurance. It is good in the sense that, if you become sick or injured, you will have health coverage. Look at the different levels of coverage, however. A plan with a $100 deductible is going to cost you more in premiums than a catastrophic policy. And because you are self-employed, your insurance rates will be higher because you will be on an individual plan instead of a group plan. Once you hire employees, you can build a group policy, but it will still cost you. Look at all your options when considering a health care plan. Typically state-run agencies have better rates.

From the Trenches

When starting your own business, don't quit your current job for at least six to twelve months. You will need the health insurance your current job provides as well as the "steady" income. Continuing to work at your current job will also allow you to purchase some equipment by using the money you make at your painting business. Working both jobs won't be easy. You will probably be giving up weekends and several evenings throughout the week, but once you are established, you will be glad you did it this way.

- *Disability Insurance:* Unfortunately, you won't be able to get disability insurance when you first start your business. First, insurance companies are hesitant to insure a company that will have unstable earnings for the first few years, as all new businesses have, and second, adjusters may have difficulty verifying claims of injury.

After your business is a few years old and you can show longevity and stability, you can apply. Long-term contracts, employees, and a strong financial statement will all be in your favor then.

- *Workers' Compensation:* At first, you probably won't need workers' compensation insurance. Businesses carry this insurance for their employees. Workers' comp covers an employee if he is injured on the job. Requirements vary from state to state, so check with your state insurance commissioner's office to find out what your state requires. Some states don't require workers' comp for companies with three to five employees. Think about the ramifications of not carrying workers' comp if you have employees and are in a state that doesn't require it. If an employee is hurt on the job, you may be sued for injury and loss of wages. Rates vary so investigate all your options.

- *Bonding:* Bonding is a type of insurance you get toward a job. Ten or fifteen years ago, bonding wasn't required. Today, some states and construction companies require you to bond. In extreme cases, they require you to bond or present a letter that says you can bond before you can bid on a job.

    There are several types of bonds. A bid or proposal bond is a bond an owner or contractor requires a subcontractor to provide to turn in bids for jobs. These types of bonds give assurance that the subcontractor has submitted a bid in good faith, will enter into a contract for the bid amount, and is able to purchase a performance bond. A minimum average premium on these types of bonds begins at $200 annually.

    A performance bond is a bond that states, in simplest terms, that the contractor or subcontractor will perform and complete the work as bid and will pay laborers, employees, vendors, and/or material suppliers. This type of bonding is becoming more common today. Home builders, owners of large homes, and apartment complex managers are requesting more and more than contractors be bonded before they start work.

    The price for a performance bond varies. It typically depends on the size of the bond, type, and your credit risk. On average it runs a percentage of the bid amount you have given for a job. For instance, if you bid $50,000 for a job, depending on your credit risk, you may have to pay 1 to 8 percent on a bond, making your premium $500 to $4,000. Most jobs under $10,000 don't require performance bonds. All bond rates vary. An insurance agent who covers workers' comp can typically help you with bonds.

Once you have your equipment ready, your office set up or in the works, your bank account opened, and insurance matters taken care of, it's time to get started on the work itself and your first job.

The First Job

Congratulations! You have your first job. This is the time for you to develop good work habits and start building your reputation. There are several steps you should take before you begin the job, during the job, and after the job is finished. For the sake of space, we will pretend this is a one-day job and you will be painting your client's living room. Following is an overview on how to make this first job a success:

- Your *bid/estimate* was approved and signed by your client. It's important that everyone is clear about the price. A written estimate is a vital and important part of your business. If you don't provide a written estimate, your customer can come back and say the price was different. By giving him the estimate and having him sign it, you can be assured there won't be any misunderstanding. Make a double copy of the estimate. After signing, you keep a copy and he keeps a copy.

Face the Facts

There will be clients who will be difficult to collect from or who will bounce checks. Be prepared. Have an attorney or a paralegal available in case you need to file a lien. If your customer's check bounces, call and arrange a time when you can go by and pick up cash.

- *Expectations.* It is important that both you and the client are up front with your needs. If the house you are painting has furniture sitting around and against the wall, have the client move it away from the wall before you arrive. A client should not expect you to move a 500-pound hutch by yourself. If you tell the client not to worry about the furniture, you need to have a system for moving it or someone to help you. You don't want to arrive on the job and not be able to start.

  Be clear about what time you will arrive. Don't say 7:00 a.m. and then arrive at 9. Be prompt. Get in, get your work done, and get out.

What to Take on a Job Checklist

❏ Brushes

❏ Rollers

❏ Drop Cloth

❏ Ladders

❏ Putty Knife

❏ Caulk Gun

❏ Caulk

❏ Masking Tape

❏ Rags

❏ Empty Bucket

❏ Paint Grate

❏ Paint for Job

■ *Bring your own tools.* I realize everyone forgets things now and then, but you can't afford to do so on your first job. Check the night before to make sure you have rags, a screwdriver, and anything else you might need. If you need a ladder and haven't had funds to buy one, borrow or rent one the night before. A small checklist is provided above so you can be sure you have everything you will need.

■ *Make sure the color is right.* Your client will probably decide on a paint color by looking at a small paint chip. Once the color has been chosen, it would be wise to make a larger sample to show your client. Sometimes paint on a chip is lighter or darker once it is spread on a larger area. You don't want to paint an entire room and then have your client think the color is too dark or too light. You can even go over and put some color on a wall the day before to be sure.

If the paint has to be ordered, don't wait until a few days before you start the job. Order it early so you will have it when you are ready to begin. Don't worry if you have to return the paint after your sample because the client doesn't like it. The paint store can sell the unopened paint cans off the shelves and the opened can as a second.

- *Be professional.* Be neat. Put your drop cloths down, tape off windows and door frames, don't splatter paint, and if you do, clean it up. Don't drink alcohol on the job, and if you smoke, go outside. Do not smoke inside someone's home, new or occupied. Clean up when the job is over. Take your rags, empty paint buckets, and dirty brushes with you. You can dispose of your trash when you get home unless there is a Dumpster onsite. If it is new construction, there will typically be a Dumpster you can use. Clean your brushes when you get home.

- *Invoicing.* When the day is over, and you have loaded your tools and equipment, make out an invoice and hand it to your client if he or she is available. If not, make it out and drop it in the mail on your way home or the next day. You will need to give the job a title, so you can choose a phrase like Job 1 or Smith Home. This will allow you to keep better track of your jobs. Some painters choose to use the address or phone number of a job. Use whichever you prefer and whatever is easiest for you.

- *Taking your cut.* After you get your check in the bank, you can finally get paid. There are certain costs you will need to subtract before you get your cut. You need to remember to deduct the cost of the paint, 33.3 percent for taxes, and 10 percent for insurances.

    Let's look at this with numbers. Say you gave your customer a bid of $600 to paint his ten-by-fifteen-foot living room and ceiling. The paint cost you $60 (three gallons at $20 each). You take your 33.3 percent out for taxes, which is $200 and then 10 percent for your insurances, which is $60. Your take should be $280 or $35 an hour for an eight-hour job.

    In chart form on page 57 is a breakdown of your deductions and costs. Keep a copy of this information in the job file for future reference.

Breakdown of Your Deductions

Job: Smith Job   **Bid Amount: $600.00**

Paid on 11/1/11 $600.00

   −33.3 percent taxes $200.00

   −10 percent insurance $60.00

   −cost of paint (three gallons @ $20.00) $60.00

                                    —————

Total pay to you $280.00

 Or $35 for an eight-hour job.

04

Writing the Business Plan

Business plan, the very words bring poundings in the head and a pain in the gut. Many shy away from and are terrified of putting together a forty-plus-page report. It reminds them too much of their school days. And I know what you're thinking. *Do I really need a business plan? Friends of mine who have started their businesses don't have a business plan.* While it's true that some businesses have started and grown without a business plan, there are many more that have business plans. Is a business plan a magic potion for success? No. There are many businesses out there that had business plans and failed.

You might think you don't need a business plan because your business is small and right now all you have is you, but if you intend to stay in this particular field, a business plan can be a blueprint or road map to help your business grow. You wouldn't build a house without a blueprint, showing where the plumbing, electrical lines, and telephone go. You wouldn't go on a long trip without a road map. Building and growing a business works on the same principles as a road map and a blueprint. A business plan is a guide that can show you what you're going to need on your journey. Building a business plan will help you learn more about the type of business you are in and the potential for reaching your goals.

Besides being a guide for you, a business plan will be needed if you are going to apply for loans. Bankers like to review business plans before they consider lending money. Investors want business plans so they know you have given thought to your business. Investors rarely invest in something if they don't believe they will recoup their money. By putting together a sound business plan, you will be one step ahead of your competitors.

Don't set a time limit on when to complete your business plan. It will take longer than an afternoon and may take anywhere from two to three weeks to two to three months. But don't let time put you off. You are not in a race. Consider a business plan an investment. Here's what a business plan can do for you:

- Help you clarify your business goals.
- Look at your business objectively; see if what you want to do is feasible and if it will make you money in the long run.
- Help you investigate the expansion of your business—what will it take, how much will it cost, and will you be able to recoup those costs.
- Point out your strengths and weaknesses.
- Identify your competitors and describe your customers.
- Help you determine your future business plans.

If the size of a business plan makes your palms sweaty, calm down. A business plan is no great mystery. It just seems big because it has so many components. A business plan consists of a cover page, a table of contents, a statement of purpose or executive summary, a company description, services offered and description of those services, a marketing plan, a plan of operation, management summary, personal financial statement, start-up expenses and capital, a financial plan, a personal résumé and the résumés of partners (if applicable), letters of recommendation, and copies of relevant contracts if needed. This chapter will break down these elements, so it will not be so overwhelming. We will look at each section, working with questions you can ask yourself to fill in your business plan as well as some suggestions for when you get stuck.

As you work on your business plan, I suggest making a file on your computer for it and also using a file folder to hold all your notes, rough drafts, and compiled

Tips That Make Cents

If you find that reading through the business plan section makes you dizzy or you think your time will be better spent on a job site or you are so busy you feel you may never get around to putting together a business plan, check out www .123easybusinessplans.com. This website offers a book for $25 that will assist you in developing a business plan by having you fill in blank spaces. If starting from scratch is making you uneasy, and you know you need a business plan but don't have a clue where to start, check this tool out. If for you, time is money . . .

❏ Cover Sheet

❏ Table of Contents

❏ Statement of Purpose or Executive Summary

❏ Company Description

❏ Services Offered and Description of Those Services

❏ Marketing Plan

❏ Operational Plan

❏ Management Plan

❏ Personal Financial Statement

❏ Start-Up Expenses and Capital

❏ Financial Plan

❏ Personal Résumé (and résumés of partners if applicable)

❏ Letters of Recommendation

❏ Relevant Contracts (copies)

information. By keeping everything in one place, you will have easy access to it and will speed the process along.

Above you will find a checklist to make sure you have covered all the areas needed. After putting everything together, mark off what you have completed on the checklist, so you'll know if you are missing anything.

Cover Sheet

Let's start with something simple. A cover sheet is fairly straightforward. It is like the title page of a book. It gives some very basic information about your business.

About one-third down the page, you need to center your business's name and then underneath it type "Business Plan." You should **bold** these two lines and make the font at least two sizes larger than the rest of your information. While you might feel you should use a different font, use Times New Roman. It is the standard for business.

Skip down to the bottom third of the page and to the left side, put the owner's name, under that the name of the business, and below that any pertinent contact information for the business, like address, city, state, zip, phone number, fax number, website URL (if applicable), and e-mail address.

Table of Contents

When all is said and done, you will need to put a table of contents together for your business plan. You will take all the subheads in this chapter, for instance, Executive Summary, Company Description, etc., list them on the left side of a sheet of paper and then put the page number where those sections begin on the right. It will be just like a table of contents in a book. I recommend you do this at the end because there may be some sections you combine, leave out, or add.

Executive Summary or Statement of Purpose

This summary will be the first item people will see when they look at your business plan. The Small Business Administration (SBA) calls this section the executive summary. It is also referred to as a statement of purpose.

Whatever you call it, it need only be two pages or less. No more than two pages. The first part or paragraph of this summary is an introduction to your business. If you have ever done any selling, consider this your five-minute sell. Some people recommend that you consider it to be like a five-minute interview pitch. Writers call it the "elevator pitch." Your goal here is to cover as much information about your business as you can in as little space as possible. You may also consider it your general overview. This summary needs to be to the point and professional.

In this section, tell the reader who the owners of the business are, who your customers are, where you are located, what your business does, and what the future looks like for your business and for the industry you are in. If you are applying for a loan, you need to state in this summary how much money you want, what the money is to be used for, how it will help your business grow, and how the money will be repaid.

Be confident when you write this section. Avoid words like maybe, not sure, hope, or perhaps. State clearly and with conviction what you know about your business and what you want and need. One thing business owners will tell you is to never seem unsure about your business. When people, especially bankers and investors, look at a business, they want to see that you are committed to this business. When they lend money or invest, they are committing themselves to it. Think about it from their perspective. Would you want to lend money or invest in a company in which the owner said, "I'm going to try to make this business work" or "I'm going to try to repay you"? I would hope not.

Since this is meant to be a summary of your business and your business needs, you might want to write this section last. That will give you time to think about what you want to include, and that message should be cohesive and complete. When adding it to your table of contents, call this section what you feel most comfortable with: executive summary or statement of purpose.

An example follows:

Quality Painters, a home-based house painting business specializing in new, restored, and renovated houses, was established in 2001. It is located in Hometown, Oklahoma. Ken Pritchard is the owner of the company and has been painting houses since 1995. Quality Painters wants to borrow $75,000 to expand our painting business to purchase equipment, add additional square footage to our shop, and hire another painter.

With this money, Quality Painters will be able to do jobs more quickly and be more cost-efficient. The ladders and airless sprayers we need will cost around $10,000. This new equipment will cut the paint time for one job in half, and one painter can be on one job while another painter can be at another location. We will be purchasing a dependable used truck. The current one we are looking at costs $18,000. Using $25,000, we will expand the shop to allow for better storage and we will be able to spray cabinets and furniture there, thus expanding our current business to include refinishing furniture.

As we plan to hire another painter, part of this money will be used to pay insurance and start-up wages. We will be using $5,000 for advertising in addition to what we currently do, as well as purchasing a sign for our shop location.

Company Description

In this section, you will put together information about the inner workings of your company, like your management team, company operations, company objectives, company goals, business philosophy, ownership, information on your industry, and marketing. Most information included here will be summaries. You will expand on these summaries in later sections.

Start off by stating what kind of business you are in and what you do. Here you can give a brief history of your business, your company location, and legal form of business your company has taken: sole proprietorship, partnership, corporation, or limited liability corporation (LLC). You also need to tell why you selected this type of legal business form.

Next, you will write your company's mission statement. This typically runs thirty words or fewer. In it you will explain your company's reason for being and its guiding standards. The mission statement needs to be simple and to the point, and it should reflect your company's personality and values. For example a paint company's mission statement might read like this:

> Quality Painters treats its clients' projects like its own, providing a cost-effective, superior paint job in less time and excellent customer service.

Take some time to thinking about your mission statement, check out examples, and write more than one. Once you have them written, think about each one. Wait a few weeks before you decide which to use. You want to make sure it accurately reflects your company because once the statement is written, you can use it on business cards, your website, and any other advertising you might do.

Next, you will move on to your company's goals and objectives. Goals are the end of the trip. Objectives are what you reach while you're working toward your goals. So, state your goals and then explain how you are going to get there.

In the following section, you will discuss your business philosophy. What is important to you about your business? About business in general? Do you like being independent? Have you always wanted to own your own business? Why?

Marketing is a major part of any business no matter what it is. Briefly state here to whom you are marketing your services. Who are your customers? Where do they live—upper-class, middle-class neighborhoods? Are they men or women? Married or single? How old are they? Why do these people want your services?

Now, describe your company's industry. Is it growing or shrinking? What changes—like trends, technology, or government regulations—do you see in the industry? Will these changes be short term or long term? How will these changes propel your industry forward? What is your company doing now to be ready for those changes?

Finally, in this section you need to discuss your company's strengths. What qualities will make your company succeed? How is your company the same as your competition? How is it different? How is your business better? What assets do you bring to your business? What kind of experience and skills do you have in painting? How do you make your company better? In other words, what makes you special in your company? What do you bring to the painting business that others can't?

Services

You have already stated what you do in other sections of the business plan, but now you are going to specifically describe your services and your fee or pricing for each service. You might try writing a general paragraph about your services, discussing what will give you the competitive edge or limit you as compared with other painting companies. Perhaps an edge would be that you are small so you can give your clients great personal service. Being small could also be a limitation because you can't take on as many jobs as bigger companies. After you finish with your paragraph, make a chart stating what your services are, a description of those services, and how much you charge.

Marketing Plan

A marketing plan is essential to any business, whether big or small. In a sentence, a marketing plan is how you intend to sell your services and to whom. Getting a clear understanding about marketing and putting it in your plan will show how you expect to reach clients and expand that client base. It will show that you know who your customers are, how to reach them, and how to keep them loyal to your services.

This is one section of your business plan that you don't want to skimp on. It is vitally important because financiers and investors will look closely at this section. They will want to know if your area of business is growing or drying up, who it is you are targeting for your business services, how you intend to present these services, how you plan to manage your clients, how you will price your services, and how you plan to handle follow-up and customer service.

When writing your marketing plan, you will want to be specific. Statistical information and sources are important as well as figures like how many house painting businesses are in your area.

To do an effective marketing plan, you will need to do research. While you may be groaning right now, research is not as difficult as you may think if you break it down. Your main goal will be to find primary and secondary resources for your research.

Primary sources involve you and the information you gather, like finding out who your competitors are and the area you are targeting. Secondary sources are resources you gather from printed publications, websites, and organizations like unions, chambers of commerce, and government agencies like the U.S. Department of Labor, Occupational Safety and Health Administration (OSHA, http://osha.gov) and the Chemical Safety Board (CSB, www.csb.gov). Your local library will also be a resource for abundant information gathering. The librarian will be more than happy to point you in the right direction and help you delve into the business resource section.

The Economics of Your Business

This will be the first part of your marketing plan, and as such you will be analyzing your market area and looking at the current facts about house painting. Your goal in this section is to present the size, trends, growth potential, barriers, and opportunities for your business.

Work through the following questions to get started on your analysis:

- *How big is your potential market?* In other words, how many houses or housing units like condos and apartments are there in your vicinity? Your local public works department or real estate office should have these numbers.

- *What is the current demand in your area?* How many houses, apartments, and condos in your area need to be painted? Is there new construction in your area? Are there older homes being refurbished? Perhaps there has been a disaster and house painters will be needed when people start rebuilding their homes? Look in the business section of your local paper. Many times you can find leads to where construction is happening or is going to happen.
- *What are the growth trends in your market?* Is there a need for more painters in your area?
- *What is the growth potential and opportunity for your business?* Are there new housing subdivisions in your area? Are there a limited number of painters available?
- *What obstacles do you face in building your business?* What kind of capital do you need for additional equipment? What kind of training and skills do you think you need? Do clients in your area trust house painters or are you going to have to rebuild trust? Is there a union in your area that requires house painters to join? Is there something unique about other local house painters that might hinder your company's growth? Is there a push in your area to use only "green" products?
- *What will you do to overcome these obstacles?* You may not be able to knock out all of them, but you can at least address 25 percent. For instance, you could go to a workshop or school to learn new skills or receive additional training. You could join a local union. You could learn about green products, what they are, how much they cost, and how to

From the Trenches

Watch construction and economic trends. Marshall, who paints in Michigan, suggests that you become an economic forecaster for your business. By looking ahead at trends, both good and bad, you can decide which direction to steer your business. For instance, if business is picking up, work all you can and save extra cash. If business appears to be slowing down, what can you do differently to keep yourself in the game? Learn a new paint skill? Specialize in something specific like asbestos removal?

Around the Paint Bucket

Don't neglect talking with other contractors like plumbers, electricians, and dry-wall installers. Find out what they are hearing about the construction business, what new regulations are being enacted, what new fees are being charged, and who is reliable in paying their subs. This can save you from big headaches down the road.

apply them. Build loyalty and trust in clients by doing a good job and offering excellent customer service before, during, and after the job.

■ *How would a change in the economy, government regulations (federal or local), or technology affect your business, and how can you prepare to handle any changes?* If there is a downturn in the economy, can your company survive, or are you so heavily in debt you may have to file bankruptcy? If you need to get a special license or go to an OSHA class, do you have the time and money to do so? Can your company go "green"?

Next, you need to describe the services you offer. A good place to start is by making a list. You can begin by listing exterior and interior and then adding what you do in these two areas. Under your exterior list you might include something like, paint garage doors, exteriors doors, balconies, porches, walls, and soffits. On your interior list you can put walls, doors, cabinets, wood floors, and whatever specialty areas you might paint. Don't forget to include texturing walls and ceilings, and any specialty finishes you might do. Other services you might want to include are sanding, scraping, refinishing wood, stripping cabinets and repainting them, etc.

When you complete your list, go back and describe the features and benefits of your services. For example, an exterior that is painted with a certain quality and color of paint is a feature. The benefits of using quality-grade paint and a pleasing color are that the exterior will look nice and fit well into the neighborhood and won't have to be painted as often.

Also under services you need to explain what kind of "after" services you will offer, like follow-up, touch-up, a service warranty, a discount on next paint job, or a service plan.

Customers or Clients

In this section you will identify and describe specifically who will be purchasing your services. You will build a demographic profile of your clients, which will include information like age, gender, and geographic location. This section of your business plan may change every six months depending on where building or renovation is happening in your area, so update this section as needed.

Let's look at the specific information you need to include and why that information is important. Look for this information at your local library or at the building code enforcement office of your city. It can sometimes also be found on your city's official website.

You will want to include the age group your business is targeting. This is important to know for target advertising. You will advertise differently for people ages thirty to fifty than you will for those under thirty or above fifty.

- *Will your client base be male or female? Married or single?* Perhaps your client base will include both genders and married, single, and divorced clients. If so, mention that your services can be rendered to all who need a quality paint job.
- *Where will your clients be located?* What part of your city or area? You can give a general description of this by saying that your client base is located in the "northwest part of the city." Next, include why your client base is or will be located there. Perhaps there is a building boom in that location or maybe a tornado blew away homes and now they are being rebuilt.
- *What is their income level?* You don't have to list specific levels. An average of $100,000 to $250,000 is sufficient for this analysis.
- *What are their social class, educational background, and occupations?* Are you looking for clients in middle- or upper-class neighborhoods? Do your clients have a college degree? What kind of jobs do they have? Are they executives? Blue-collar workers? Educated professionals? Your advertising efforts will be different for different classes of clients. For instance, upper-class clients will want to know you are a professional and will do a good job in their home. In addition to a quality job, middle-class clients might be looking for a price break, maybe a coupon to get a discount.
- *What are their beliefs?* Do your clients consider having a nice house a status symbol? Do they live in a neighborhood that has standards for its homes? Is there a neighborhood association that requires a paint job every few years?

All of these factors are important when looking at demographics. Don't skimp or skip any of these areas. These figures are typically easy to find. Check on the Internet, or with your local library, city hall, or local real estate agent.

Competition

This is an important part of your marketing plan because you need to know who you will be competing against for clients. If there are one hundred house painters who have your area sewn up, you may need to rethink your business or your location. However, if only two or three painters are in your area and there are thousands of potential clients, you have a better chance of picking up quite a bit of work.

First, you will need to identify your competition. List the local house painting contractors in your area. Include their addresses, what their specific area of expertise is, how many painters they have working for them, and how long they have been in business.

Next, you are going to work on answering three questions: How is my business similar to my competitors, how is my business different from my competitors, and how will my business be better? You can also think of it as describing you and your company's advantages and disadvantages.

For these three questions you can look at your competitors' pricing, quality of work, and services they offer. Are they reliable? Is the company and its workers stable? What kind of expertise do the workers have? What is the company's reputation? What about the workers' appearance on the job? Do they dress neatly, or are they sloppy and dirty? Does this company advertise regularly? What kind of image does it project in the community?

Once these questions are answered, you will write three summary paragraphs including all the information you have gathered for *each* of your competitors. Typically you will have one-half to one page of information per competitor.

It may help if you make a chart similar to the one on page 70 to keep all your information together. Add columns for additional competitors and additional questions you feel need to be answered. Each square may need to be increased in size to hold the information you glean. Use this chart when answering your three questions on each competitor.

Now that you have gathered all your information and you are more informed about your industry, your customers, and your competition, you should have a clear

Competition Analysis Chart

Questions to Answer	Your Business	Name of Competitor	Name of Competitor	Name of Competitor
Age of business				
Services offered				
Quality of work				
Pricing—Give numbers for specific services				
Is pricing high, low, or competitive?				
Is the company reliable?				
What is the company's reputation?				
What level and type of expertise does the company have?				
Does the company advertise? If so, how?				
Describe the workers' appearance. Do they dress neatly, or are they sloppy?				
What image does the company project in the community?				
Does the company take credit cards, personal checks, cash, or all three?				

vision of where your business fits in the house painting arena. Think about what is unique about your business as compared with other house painting businesses, how your services are rendered, what specific advantages your business offers, and write a paragraph about it. This will be the brand, niche, or position your company holds in your clients' minds. For example, instead of running late on jobs and dragging out the job for two weeks, you go in and get a quality job done in three days. After getting several jobs under your belt, your clients may see you as "the best and fastest painter in town" and tell their friends and neighbors.

Your Marketing Strategy

The next step is to outline a marketing strategy for your business. This is done by getting word out to people about your business. If you are not promoting or telling people about your business, there is no way they can know you are in business. So, you need to think about how you want people to know about you.

The first step in promotion is thinking about how you want to contact people. What kind of media will you be using? Business cards? Word of mouth? Flyers? Ads in the local paper? Attending trade shows? Think about why you are choosing these types of media, and consider how often you will use this approach. How will this approach help your business grow?

Since your business may be a new one, television and even newspaper ads may be too expensive. Don't overlook low-cost types of advertisement. Consider writing a press release for the local paper. Many times local papers will take your press release and run it to introduce a new business to the community. Talk to other home-based business owners and find out what kind of low-cost advertising they do. Sometimes, several businesses will pull together and put together a promotional campaign on their own.

What kind of business image do you want your customers to see? Since you are in a service business and run a business out of your home, you don't have to worry about clients coming to your office, but you do need to worry about your image when you or your business is out there. What kind of logo do you have planned? What does your logo say about your business? When people see your business card, proposals, invoices, brochures, and signage on your truck, can they immediately identify it as your company?

Do you have a website? Let's face it, businesses need websites. Give someone a card, and he will be curious about who you are, what you do, and how much you charge to paint a room. If you are not immediately available to answer those questions, a client will want to visit your website. If you don't have a website, your prospective client may not take the initiative to call. The second-most frequently asked question today after "Do you have a card?" is "Do you have a website?"

How much money do you have or how much are you willing to spend on a promotional budget? You will need to figure out how much you will be spending at the start of your business and then for ongoing promotion. Your initial cost will no doubt be your biggest budgetary concern, with the purchase of business cards, a website, proposals, invoices, etc. If you schedule a budget for promotion, you will be able to continue to reach your current clients and new ones as well.

Your Pricing

In this section, you will explain how you set your prices. You may think that setting the lowest price would be a good approach in the beginning. That's not always the case. You need to think about your profit margin. Setting a price that is about average is a good policy. You should try to compete on the services that you offer and the quality of those services. If you give people a good job in a timely manner, most won't squabble about prices, and besides, a large painting company could probably undercut you anyway.

Next, compare your prices with those of your competitors. Are you higher? Lower? About the same? Aim for the middle ground. Consider your thought process when you get a bid. Most people won't go with the highest bid or the lowest price. The lowest price makes them think of the adage, "You get what you pay for." Most clients will look for the middle ground. They want a good job at a reasonable price.

Do you have a discount policy like offering coupons or discounts on referrals? How often do you run your discount offer? Typically, what is the discount amount? Ten percent? Fifteen?

How do you collect or plan on collecting your money? Do you immediately bill your client? Bill in thirty days? What is your policy for late payments? Do you accept credit cards?

Selling Your Services

Finally, you need to describe how you sell your services. Being a house painter, you look at jobs or at blueprints and turn in a bid or a proposal to prospective clients. Explain the steps you take in doing this, from the initial phone call to turning in the bid.

The Sales Forecast

This will be included at the end of your marketing plan section. Now that you have investigated your clients, your services, and your marketing strategy, you will need to put actual numbers to your plan. This is done by making a sales forecast projection. It is typically done month by month. When working on the sales forecast, you might want to do two—a best-case scenario and a worst-case scenario.

Let's look at the thinking process in a best-case scenario. You and a two-man crew go through two existing houses per week at $2,000 per house and one new 2,500-square-foot house per month at $10,000. Income for the month would be eight total existing houses (two per week for four weeks) multiplied by $2,000 ($16,000) plus $10,000 for the new house, or $26,000 minus expenses. Expenses may run around $4,000, giving you a base profit of $22,000.

In a worst-case scenario, you are the only painter and can only do one existing house per week or a couple of living rooms at $1,200 a week and a new 2,500-square-foot house every two months making your income from the new house $5,000 a month. That would make your monthly income $9,800 ($1,200 x 4 weeks = $4,800 + $5,000), less $2,000 in expenses to bring your base profit to $7,800.

Maybe in six months you are looking to hire a few more painters, doubling the business in your best-case scenario by painting four existing houses per week and two new 2,500-square-foot houses per month. You can add that to your sales forecast.

The worksheet on page 74 will help you as you fill out your own.

You may have several other painters at this point, or you may be getting ready to hire. By doing a best-case scenario and a worst-case scenario, you can see where your business sits and where it can go. Don't worry about exact numbers, just get as close as you can. Keep your notes and figures for future reference. You might want to think about making several of these spreadsheets, one for your final projection and one for worksheets. Throughout the year, you can adjust your numbers according to the work you get, and the men you hire. You can develop a history of your business much the same way, except that you will be working the numbers backward.

Operational Plan

In this section of your business plan, you are going to explain how your business or company operates, your location, your equipment, who works for you, and your work

Sales Forecast Worksheet

	Example	Jan	Feb	March	April	May	June
1) Money in bank at Start of Month	5,000						
2) Money from Existing Houses 1 and 2	4,000						
3) Money from Existing Houses 3 and 4	4,000						
4) Money from Existing Houses 5 and 6	4,000						
5) Money from Existing Houses 7 and 8	4,000						
6) Money from New House	10,000						
7) Totals for Month (Add 2, 3, 4, 5, 6)	26,000						
8) Expenses	4,000						
9) Salaries Paid	9,600						
10) Total Pay–Outs (Add 8 and 9)	13,600						
11) Profit for Month (Subtract 10 from 7)	12,400						
12) Bank Total (Add 1 and 11)	17,400						

methods. Since you are a home-based business and perhaps a one-man show, you can start by writing a paragraph about how you handle the services you provide and customer service. Do you wait for people to call you, or do you call leads? When you get a lead, what is your follow-through? When the job is finished, if someone has a complaint, how do you handle it?

Next, write a few paragraphs about where your office is located and why you chose a home-based business. Here is a good place to put the amount you deduct from your taxes for your expenses—rent, insurance, maintenance, and utilities. This is also the space to explain where you store your equipment and why. You can then explain how most of your day is spent on a job site and how you use your office for support.

You need to include information on the types of permits you are required to get (if any), insurance coverage you are required to keep, any licenses and bonds you have to purchase, government restrictions and regulations like environmental, health, or workplace laws, and any other regulations relating to the painting industry. These will be included under a Legal Environment section in the operational plan. Describe each of these areas, telling what these items are for, how much they cost, and how they benefit your business.

Next, you will discuss your personnel, if you have any. You will tell the number of employees you have and/or how many more you want to employ, what type of work they do, and how skilled they are at that work. If you have a secretary in addition to your painters, you will discuss her role in the business as well. You will also explain how you pay your employees, what your hiring requirements are, how you train your employees for the job, and if you have a probationary period for those you hire. Also include job descriptions for each worker, explaining who does what, and discuss the hours you and your employees work, and your company employment policy. (Writing a company policy will be covered in chapter 6.)

After explaining your employment structure, you will discuss your inventory and suppliers. First, let's look at the inventory, if you keep any. You will, of course, keep supplies for your business like rags and cleaning supplies. If you keep some paint on hand or you have purchased paint and retain gallons after a job is complete, then this will be figured into your inventory list. What is the average value of your inventory? Explain why you keep inventory on hand. As a service company, explaining your inventory makes good sense and will show an investor or banker that you have given thought about what you keep on hand.

Now, who are your suppliers, and where do you get your paint, equipment, and other supplies? You should list their names and addresses, their history with you (how long have you been doing business with them), the type and amount of paint and equipment each one provides, their credit and delivery services, how reliable they are, whether they always have the paint you need and how quickly they can get it if they don't. You will also include information about the costs of your supplies. Are they going up or down or remaining steady? If costs are rising, how are you dealing with the increase now and in the future?

Also in this section, you need to discuss your *Credit Policies*. If you require payment immediately after the job, you can write "nonapplicable" or "does not extend credit" in this section.

If you do work on a credit basis, you will discuss your procedures and policies. Is extending credit customary in your field? How much credit do you extend? To whom? How do you check a person's credit? What are your credit terms? What is the method of payback? How much interest do you charge? When is payment due? What do you charge when payment is late? Do you offer a discount for prompt payment or cash payment? What does it cost you to extend credit and have you figured that into the overall cost of a job?

If you extend credit, you should be keeping some form of record of payment. You will explain that next. How many days do you let payment go for slow-paying clients before you send a reminder, call them, or contact an attorney or credit agency? Also, how much of your working capital is tied up in these credit accounts? On the flip side, what do you owe your suppliers? Are you paying any of them late? If so, how late and why?

Management Plan

This section will explain who will do the day-to-day managing of the business. If you are the only employee, you can write a paragraph about what you bring to the business, what you do, and what special skills you have, if any. If you have employees, list each one by name (typically by seniority level), the position they hold in the business, what they bring to the business, and the tasks they perform. If you are looking for a loan or trying to get investors, include your résumé and the résumé of key people in the business. Also include your plan for the continuation of the business should you die or are incapacitated in some way.

Next you will want to list any professional or advisory support you may have for the business. This can include a banker, an accountant, an insurance agent or agents, an attorney, consultants, and/or mentors. You should give their contact information: name, address, phone number, e-mail, how long you have been doing business with them, and what they do or bring to your business.

Personal Financial Statement

Supplying a personal financial statement is standard for all businesses. This will list your assets (what you own whether paid for or not) and liabilities (your debts) that are not included in the business and how much you are worth personally. As a small business owner, you may have to draw on your personal assets like your home or personal vehicles to get financing for your business. A personal financial statement will show what is available. Banks as well as investors will always ask for this information. If you have an accountant, which is strongly recommended, he should be able to print you a statement quickly. The Small Business Administration has a blank form you can fill out to create your own personal financial statement at http://www .ct.gov/dot/lib/dot/documents/ddbe/personal_financial_statement_sba.pdf. Use the worksheet on page 78 to fill out your personal financial information and then transfer it to a formal statement.

Start-Up Expenses and Capital

No matter what type of business you could start, you would have expenses. A start-up house painting business may not have as many beginning expenses as some other business, but you will have expenses. Some expenses will be more than you anticipated. Planning ahead and doing careful research will help you keep your expenses down until you can gain more capital to buy more equipment and hire more workers.

If you don't know exactly how much money you are going to need to get started or expand, pad your figures. SCORE recommends that you should add at least 20 percent to what you perceive to be your total start-up expenses. When you are figuring out how much money you will need, more is always better.

Be as accurate as you can with your figures. A good rule of thumb is to list everything you think you might need, even down to the paper clips. After you have decided all you need, you will have to explain why your business will need specific

Personal Financial Worksheet

ASSETS	DOLLAR AMOUNT	LIABILITIES	DOLLAR AMOUNT
Cash in Banks		Accounts Payable	
Savings Account		Notes Payable to Banks and Others (credit cards, etc.)	
Retirement Funds (IRA or other)		Auto Balance Owed (total)	
Accounts Receivable		Mortgage Balance on Real Estate (total)	
Life Insurance-Cash Surrender Value Only		Life Insurance Payment (yearly payment)	
Stocks and Bonds		Other Installment Accounts (Total owed)	
Real Estate		Unpaid Taxes	
Vehicle(s) Present Value		Other Liabilities	
Other Personal Property		Total Liabilities	
Other Assets		Net Worth (Take Total Assets from other side and put here.)	
Total Assets		Total (Subtract Liability Total from Net Worth.)	
Salary		As Endorser or Co-Maker	
Other Income		Legal Claims and Judgments	

items. If you have a loan for an airless sprayer, for instance, you will need to disclose that information. If you are looking to buy an airless, make sure you include the make and model, how much it will cost, whether the place you are buying it from has terms for financing, and what those terms are.

You will also need to list your sources of capital—meaning where you are getting or can get money, like investors or banks in the form of loans.

Use the worksheet on page 79 to fill in information on start-up expenses and capital.

Start-Up Expenses and Capital Worksheet

SOURCES OF CAPITAL	
Owner's Name and Ownership Percentage	$
Other Investors	$
1)	
2)	
Bank Loans	$
Bank 1	
Bank 2	
Bank 3	
Loans (Other Sources)	$
1)	
2)	
3)	
START-UP EXPENSES	
Buildings	$
Construction	
Purchase	
Other	
Equipment	$
Brushes	
Rollers	
Ladders	
Airless Sprayers	
Furniture for Office	
Vehicle	$
Truck 1	
Truck 2	
Administration Expenses	$
Accounting Fees	
Insurance	
Legal Fees	
Office Fees	
Advertising Expenses	$
Advertising	
Signs	
Printing (Cards and Brochures)	
Other	

Financial Plan

Here, you are going to explain how much you intend to make, how much you are going to need to get started, and how much you will need to make on an ongoing basis to stay in business. Since you are a single-person business or a small business, you don't have to be as elaborate as someone who owns and runs a big company, but you do have to do your homework and make your financial plan sound.

You should include a twelve-month profit-and-loss statement, information on projected cash flow, your opening day balance sheet, and a break-even analysis. SCORE has forms for each of these categories on its website. Even if you don't use SCORE because you are a small business, you might want to take a look at what it suggests for reference. Let's take a look at each of the items you will include.

The twelve-month profit-and-loss statement is where you will plug numbers in to determine what it will take for your business to be successful. You will be looking at your gross profit against your total expenses, which will give you your net profit. Your gross profit will be the amount your business takes in. Then, you will deduct expenses like advertising, vehicle costs (loan and maintenance), telephone, rent, insurances, supplies, maintenance and repairs on equipment, accounting and legal fees, taxes, salaries, and any other expenses you can think of. Since you are a working on a projection, it is a future estimate. You will need to explain your figures and how you came to your conclusions.

Some business owners choose to do a four-year projection as well. A four-year is very rarely required for loans, but it is a good personal source to refer to. Whichever you decide, one or both, take careful notes and keep all your research in case you need to explain your projection figures. They will be good sources to refer to when you need to update your information.

Next is the cash-flow projection. In the worksheet on page 81 you will look at start-up costs, beginning expenses, operation costs, and reserves. You will need to think about when the work is completed and when you will be getting paid for each job you do. By determining how much you have coming in and how much you have going out, you will get a figure for the amount of cash flow you will have available to run your business.

When working on your cash-flow assumptions, you need to consider irregular expenses like quarterly taxes. You also should realize that you don't generally get paid for a job at the same time as when you put out money for a job. For instance, let's say you do a job at the end of October and you have to pay for the paint up

Cash Flow Projection Worksheet

	Opening Day of Business	January	February	March	April	May	June
Cash On-Hand							
Collected Receipts							
Other Money Coming In							
Total Cash Available							
Expenditures							
Purchases							
Wages							
Supplies							
Vehicle Expenses							
Equipment Maintenance and Repair							
Advertising							
Accounting Expense							
Legal Expense							
Taxes							
Insurance							
Advertising							
Loan Payments							
Miscellaneous							
Subtotal							
Owner's Withdrawal							
Total Expenditures							
Cash Position at End of Month							

> **Face the Facts**
>
> Your business will change. You may get a partner, decide to expand more quickly than you first anticipated, or buy new equipment. Review your business plan at least every eighteen months to two years and revise what needs to be changed. By keeping it up to date, your business plan will be ready to go whenever you need it.

front. If you are not going to get paid until November, this will influence your cash-flow figures.

If you need to include an opening day balance sheet, this should be a fairly easy task since you have completed the cash-flow projections. A balance sheet shows your assets, what your business has of value, and your liabilities, the business's debts. When you subtract liabilities from assets, you get what's called owner's equity. For instance, let's say you listed your business truck and your equipment as assets at a dollar figure of $50,000. You still owe $15,000 on your truck, but your equipment is clear. You would subtract $15,000 from $50,000 leaving you with an owner's equity of $35,000.

Finally, you will write a break-even analysis. This is basically a statement that predicts the amount of money you need to make to recover all the costs of the business. Make sure you include a statement backing up your figures.

Appendices

If you have been thorough in your research and gathering of materials, you should have many supporting documents. The appendix of your business plan is where these research items are placed. Some of the documents you will want to include are advertising materials like brochures, flyers, and business cards; copies of contracts you may have secured; leases on storage facilities; a detailed list of equipment owned or that needs to be purchased; market or industry studies that support your company; magazine articles that may have been written about your industry or business; resumes of you, your partner, and employees, if applicable; recommendation letters from current or future clients; and a complete list of assets that can be used as collateral when applying for a loan.

Don't worry if you don't have everything mentioned above. Put what you do have in the appendix. You can always add to or take away as needed.

Future Plans

When finished with your business plan, buy a half-inch three-ring-binder notebook and put your business plan inside. This will keep it nice and neat, and if you have to change or update anything, it will be easy to access. Also, always keep a copy of your business plan electronically. While a hard copy is fine, you may find that bankers and investors want you to send them a copy of your business plan via e-mail or electronic fax.

05

Keeping Track of Your Business

In this chapter we will look at everything from bookkeeping to overseeing clients. I know that filling out a lot of paperwork is the last thing you had in mind when you thought about starting your business. If you are like many people, your goal is to go to work, make the money, and then go home. Unfortunately running a business is a little more involved than that.

I, personally, am a very organized person. Sure, paperwork gets in the way at times of what I really want to do, but when I need records, I know I have them and where they are. Keep good records and your life will be a lot simpler. At the beginning, it will probably be a pain in the old keister, but let the Internal Revenue Service call just once and you will be glad you kept your records and kept them up to date. When there is something I don't want to do, I say to myself, "You are an adult and adults have to do certain things." There's no need complaining about or even dreading certain tasks. Just do them and move on. I've found that is the best way to handle these chores, record keeping included.

If financial bookkeeping is overwhelming for you and you can't even begin to think straight when faced with all the dos and don'ts of this chapter, consider hiring an accountant. We have had an accountant since the beginning of our business. She has been a godsend on more than one occasion. She balances the business's checkbook, figures our corporate taxes, keeps track of profit and loss statements, and takes care of any audits we may be required to do throughout the year.

The key is to get started on the right track. Once you get started and get in the habit of doing your records, it will become easier and you will become faster at it. Record keeping is the least strenuous part of your business work, but it is time-consuming at first. You're a professional now, you own your own business, so let's get started.

Keeping the Books

Everyone who owns his or her own business knows that bookkeeping is part of the whole. It's not a pleasant job, and most people dread it because it is tedious, but it has to be done. Bookkeeping is how you keep track of your business's finances. It includes your business checking account, income and expense statements, balance sheets, and more. Let's take a look at this part of your business a little closer.

Why all the fuss about keeping the books? When you run a business, the Internal Revenue Service wants to know where the money you make goes and why it goes there. There is a certain standard by which it judges whether you are in fact running a business or have a hobby, whether an expense is a business expense or a personal one. If you stuff all your receipts in a box without keeping proper records, how will the IRS know if it was a legitimate expense or if the receipt was given to you by your neighbor? Chances are the agency will throw out the questionable deduction, and when you run a business, you need all the deductions you can get.

Second, you can't remember everything. Trust me on this. *You* need to know where your money is going and why it is going there as well. Are you using your money wisely to build your business, or are you spending money right and left on items you don't need and can't afford. You need to keep track of not only where your money goes, but also who owes you what and whom you owe. Without proper records, you can get so spread out you don't know what's going on with your money.

Isn't all this record keeping going to get complicated and confusing? Not if you do it right at the beginning. For starting a business, the KISS method is always the best—**K**eep **I**t **S**ickeningly **S**imple. Later on, when you learn the ins and outs, you can make it as complicated as you want, and with growth, the hiring of employees, and so forth, it may become complicated on its own, so don't sweat it now.

How long is record keeping going to take? In the beginning, probably less than an hour a day and then an additional two to three hours a month to close out the month and reconcile all your records. But you must stay on top of it. I know when you come in at night after work, you will be tired, but get your records done. Consider it an extended part of the job. In the early days of Freedom Painting Service, David kept a file cabinet with things he needed by his recliner. He would come in, put his feet up, and work on his books while I cooked supper. Now, the books have become a little more complicated, and he has an office with a desk and two computers.

Can computers help? Yes and no, if you have the right software. Computing software for the small business is not that expensive these days, but you will have to take the time to learn to use it. Once you do, however, it can cut your bookkeeping time in half. Most programs will not only assist in keeping the books, but will also write checks and separate them into files or columns. The alternative is to build your own charts and records by using a spreadsheet program or hiring someone to help you with your bookkeeping.

Whom should I hire and when? Who and when depends on you, your business, and how fast you grow. We have never used a bookkeeper. They are expensive and we personally like knowing what our business is doing and how it is doing. When you have a bookkeeper, he or she takes care of not only your books, but also writing checks, paying bills and employees, and keeping track of where your money is going. Horror stories abound about bookkeepers stealing money from businesses. So unless you get really big and your time is freed up to stay on top of your bookkeeper, I'd advise against hiring one.

On the other hand, an accountant is someone you might not be able to do without. While a bookkeeper deals with the day's income and expenditures and logs them, an accountant takes that information and produces profit and loss statements, balance sheets, monthly statements, and tax returns. An accountant is the one who can tell you how much in taxes you can expect to pay and when to pay them, and can give you a heads-up on how your business is doing financially. A good accountant will know the tax laws and stay on top of changes, as tax laws change quite frequently. Our accountant attends seminars yearly to learn about the new tax codes and then reports back to us so we can adjust our business and income accordingly. Good accountants are not cheap; typically they run from $1,000 to $2,500 a month, but they can save you thousands of dollars in the long run.

Business Bank Account

When running a business, you must open a business checking account. This will be separate from your personal checking account. Your business account is where you will work with all your incoming and outgoing business funds. When you are paid for a job, you deposit the check in your business account, and when you pay business bills, you do it out of your business account. There are no exceptions to this rule. Conducting business this way is simple and really is in your best interest. You might want to consider getting a business debit card. This can help you because you don't have to carry around your big check ledger. Just make sure that you write down what you spent on your debit card in your checkbook as soon as you get home. If you have to pay for something out of your personal account, pay yourself back by writing a check from your business account. Make a notation about what it is for on the check and also enter that information in your check log. If you pay for something for the business in cash, pay yourself back for that expenditure as well. Keep your personal and business bills separate and pay them separately. It just makes good business sense.

Tips That Make Cents

Don't carry your checkbook around with you, and if you must take it with you, don't leave it in your work truck. Thieves are everywhere these days, and they will not hesitate to break the window of your truck to get to it. Make out your checks before you leave home, carry one in your wallet, or use your business debit card or credit card to pay for purchases.

Forget about getting cash back when you deposit a business check. The IRS requires business owners to deposit the total amount of the check into the business account. Once it is deposited, you can then write a check for the amount of cash you need.

When you are thinking about opening an account, choose a bank that doesn't require business accounts to keep a minimum balance. Sometimes, especially in the beginning, you may need money to buy supplies or pay bills. If you are required to keep a minimum $500 balance, you may find yourself in a mess.

Also, be aware that some banks require a ten-day hold for checks over a certain amount. Typically that amount is $5,000, but at the beginning of your business, if you're new to the bank, it may decide to hold $1,000 checks. We ran into this problem when we were switching banks at one point. Needless to say, we went back to our original banker, even though her branch was on the other side of town from where we lived.

Face the Facts

Balancing the Business Checkbook

Most people don't care for balancing their checkbooks. It's not difficult but can be time-consuming if the numbers are a bit off. You, no doubt, have a personal checking account, so you probably have been balancing your personal checkbook for some time now. The process is the same, but let's look at this task nonetheless.

Keep your checkbook up to date. A good habit to develop is to write down every check you write in your ledger immediately. This will save you from having problems down the road. Be sure to deduct the amount of the check from your balance as you go along. With any luck, this will keep you from running out of money before the end of the month.

Getting started. You will need to have your bank statement and your bank ledger. These days most banks don't return checks; they send them as photocopies, typically eight or ten to a sheet of paper. These checks will be in order from the lowest check number to the highest. Your statement sheet will list the checks this way as well.

Set your ledger to the right, the first page of your statement in the middle, and the photocopies of your checks to the left. Start with the first check photocopy, find it on the first statement page, put a check beside the numbers, and then find the same check number in your ledger. Some people put a line through the ledger entry, some circle the check number, and others continue to use check marks. Whichever you decide, make sure there is some indication that this check has come in.

As you go through these canceled checks, look at the amount they are written for and make sure that it matches what you have put in the ledger. If you have transposed any numbers, like writing $408.00 instead of $480.00, this will mess up your balance. It may be fine if it makes you long, but if it makes your account short, that can give you a lot of headaches. We have had both experiences, so we try to pay attention to the amount of the check and what we put in the ledger. Write down and subtract any service charges and automatic loan payments from your ledger as well if you haven't already done so.

After all the checks are marked off, mark off any debit and ATM charges and finally your deposits, making sure they are in the ledger as well as your bank statement. Now, it is time to start adjusting your numbers.

If you receive your bank statements through the mail, a form appears on the back of the first page that will help you balance your bank statement. First, you will need to write down the balance shown on your statement. Add any deposits that are not shown on the statement if you have had any and have entered them into your ledger. Next, in the space provided, write down all the outstanding checks and charges that have not come out of your bank account yet and total them. Subtract this amount from your statement balance and any service charge amount. This amount should agree with your register balance. If you receive your statement via e-mail, you will not have a form. Use the one on page 90 to balance your checkbook.

Troubleshooting: When the numbers don't match, there's no need to scream and holler about it. Just take a few deep breaths and look over your numbers again. Because bank statements are generated by computers, your balance from the bank is rarely wrong. That makes the culprit who made the mistake you. That doesn't make you a bad person. We're human, we make mistakes, and when we make them, we have to put our heads down and fix them.

The first step is to check for amounts that may be written down wrong. Maybe your subtraction or addition is off? I have found that nine times out of ten, when my numbers don't jibe, I've added or subtracted wrong. What really drives me crazy is if I'm off by pennies, but pennies can add up. So keep at it. If you let it go, the next month you may be shorter still and you don't want checks to start bouncing. The service fees alone can run into the hundreds of dollars.

If the worst happens, you can always go to your bank and open a new account, but this will cost you money. You'll have to buy new checks, get a new debit card, etc. It's best just to stay on top of your account.

Checks Outstanding Not Charged to Bank Account		Month and Year of This Statement	
Check Number	Check Amount	Balance Shown on Your Statement	$
	$	Add deposits not shown (if any) +	$
	$	TOTAL of balance and additional deposits =	$
	$	Put Outstanding Check Total Here	$
	$	Subtract Line 4 from Line 3 Put Subtotal Here	$
	$	The subtotal is your balance. Write that number here. It should agree with what is in your check registry.	$
	$		
	$		
	$		
	$		
Outstanding Check Total	$		

Business checks are larger than personal checks. They include a ledger to the left-hand side of the check where information can be written and kept track of, like what you purchased from a particular store, taxes, etc. A good way to go is to get checks and deposit slips with carbons. They may cost a little more but will be well worth the money if you are in a hurry, write a check or deposit one, and forget to put it in your ledger.

If you decide to do the bookkeeping yourself without the assistance of an accountant, balance your checkbook every month. This is one job that cannot be ignored. This will help you catch any discrepancies you may have from your writing of the check to entering the amount in your register. It will also let you catch any bogus charges deducted from your account. Once, we had two service charges subtracted. The bank was quick to rectify the overcharge, but we were glad to have caught it. Balancing your checkbook immediately will also give you a clear picture of where you stand for the month, and as a business owner, it is always prudent to know the bottom line.

Choosing Your Bookkeeping System

Let's talk accounting. While the mere word may cause you to break out in hives, accounting doesn't have to be traumatic. As a matter of fact, the simpler the accounting system, the better. There are several programs you can investigate—Quicken, Quickbooks, and Peachtree Accounting are probably the three best known. To get started, you may want to download Quickbooks, Simple Start Free Edition. Intuit puts out a new version every year, and programs are available for Windows and Mac users. It will do all the basic accounting tasks, and you can always upgrade when you need more features.

There are two basic bookkeeping methods in accounting: single entry and double entry. With single entry, you enter your figures only once per transaction. This method is simple and recommended for most home-based businesses. The double entry system has you recording each transaction twice—once as a debit and then as a credit. This system provides cross-checks for you and helps decrease errors, although it is somewhat more complicated.

Cash Versus Accrual

Just as there are two ways to do your bookkeeping, there are two ways to keep track of your incoming and outgoing money—cash or accrual. Using the cash method, income is reported when it is received and expenses are deducted when they are paid. With this system, credit cards and checks are managed the same way as cash. Most small businesses use this type of method. When using this method, you will want to get paid as soon as the job is complete and pay your bills as soon as they come due.

The accrual method is different in that income is reported when the transaction occurs, even if you haven't collected the money yet. For instance, if you billed Mrs. Smith for a house painting job on November 10, then that is when you would report the income even if she hasn't paid you yet. You do the same for expenses. You report and enter those when they occur, not when you pay them. It would be like charging paint at the paint store. You would enter that expense even though the bill is not paid yet. The accrual method is more complex and time-consuming, but if you need to keep a closer eye on your financial condition, this is the way to do it. Both the accrual and the cash method can be used in single-entry or double-entry accounting systems. With that said, since you are running a service business and have little inventory, your best bet will be to go with the cash method. You will need to let the IRS know which method you are using and can change methods at any time without asking permission. However, the change must be made at the beginning of the fiscal year and you must notify the IRS of the change.

Your business, because it is a small home-based business, will operate on a calendar year, which runs from January 1 to December 31. Big businesses typically operate on fiscal years, which is still a twelve-month period but can begin on a date other than January 1.

The accounting and bookkeeping methods you use will be up to you, your business, and the complexity with which your business operates. You should sit down and discuss your needs with an accountant if you aren't sure. The accountant can direct you to what will work for your business. Typically, most home-based businesses and small businesses can get by without complicated and complex financial reports. If your business stays solvent and you pay your bills on time every month, you should have a clear view of how your business is handled and where it is headed financially.

Bookkeeping Documents

With that said, let's go over a few reports all business owners should be aware of even if they have an accountant or a bookkeeper. These items will not only help you understand your business better, but they will also aid you when you put together your business plan if you haven't already done so.

- **Balance Sheets:** Balance sheets show you what your business is worth. It shows you the difference between your liabilities and your assets.
- **Cash-Flow Projections:** Your cash-flow projection will tell you where your money is going each month and whether you will have enough money to operate your business and pay your bills in the upcoming month. If you have employees, pay rent, and have other expenses, these projections will be the most important financial statements you can have. They can show you whether you need to lay people off, scale back on expenses, or get more work.
- **Profit and Loss Statements:** Profit and loss statements show you how much you are bringing in and how much you are spending in your business. If your business is making more than it is spending, then it is making a profit. If your business is spending more than it is making, your business will be taking a loss.

Income and Expenses

Now, let's take a look at your income and expenses. We'll discuss what constitutes income and what counts as expenses. The Internal Revenue Service draws a fine line between personal and business expenses. You need to know what that line is. Cross it and you could get audited, and end up paying a hefty fine or worse still, end up behind bars.

Income is pretty self-explanatory. That is the money you bring in from operating your business. You may want to separate your income into categories so you can see what kind of money you are making from each job you do. For instance, you might want to know how much money you earned from new homes versus how much from existing homes or maybe apartments. These divisions won't be necessary when you figure your taxes. All the IRS wants to know is how much you made overall, so the categories are for you. This is a good way to see where you are making the most money and perhaps where you should concentrate your efforts.

Expenses are a bit more complicated. When looking at expenses, you need to be aware of variable and fixed expenses. Also, be sure to ask an accountant which expenses are valid as deductions. There are some expenses that you can take 100 percent of as a deducation, others you can only take a percentage. Knowing the difference can save you many headaches down the road. A good rule to keep in mind is: "All expenses must be job related."

Variable Expenses

Variable expenses are ones that fluctuate from time to time. You may incur these expenses all the time, sometimes, or not at all. They may be $50 on one job and $200 on the next. These are your on-the-job-related expenses. We can break them down into the following categories:

- *Materials and Supplies:* These are expenses related to specific jobs like paint, caulk, and drywall mud. If you are doing a specialty job and you have to buy sponges that you will use for a particular part of that job, you can take off the sponges as an expense too.
- *Miscellaneous:* These are expenses on jobs that you really don't know how to categorize. Use this category until you can decide where the expense needs to go.
- *Labor:* This category is for payroll to your employees and the other costs you pay, like workers' comp, payroll taxes, health insurance, etc. Be diligent in keeping track of all of these expenses as you will need the expense divisions at the end of the year when working on your business tax reports.
- *Subcontractors:* These are expenses incurred when you bring someone else in on the job, for instance a wallpaper hanger or a mural painter. They are used and paid from one job.

Expenses

These are business-related expenses that occur regularly and typically monthly. These will be divided into regular deductions, depreciating deductions, and percentage deductions.

Regular Deductions

Regular deductions are those that occur on a regular basis—week to week, month to month, quarter to quarter, and year to year. You know you have to pay these expenses, and you typically know the amount, although the amount may change a little from time to time depending on the service.

- *Accounting:* These are expenses you pay to an accountant whether they are for figuring your monthly statements or doing your yearly tax return.
- *Advertising:* Any expense that allows you to get the word out to customers about your business: business cards, letterhead, estimate and bid sheets with your business name and logo on them, ads in newspapers, flyers, brochures, and your website.
- *Bank Charges and Fees:* If your bank has monthly fees or you have any charges, you can deduct these expenses. (Note: If your bank account earns interest, you must claim that at the end of the year as income.)
- *Dues and Subscriptions:* If you subscribe to industry magazines or pay union dues or some type of yearly organizational fees, these are tax deductible. Remember to include any monthly fee your website might cost. Typically, you will have to pay for hosting, which will need to be counted here.
- *Educational Fees:* These fees will include any classes, workshops, and seminars that you have paid for. Any manuals, books, or CDs can also be counted as educational fees as long as they relate to your business.
- *Entertainment and Food:* You may ask, "Who the heck am I going to entertain? I'm going to be working my butt off." You might be surprised. If you are negotiating with a builder or a real estate agent, you might want to take him to breakfast or lunch. These meals are deductible expenses as well as any meals you eat while working or while attending conferences, workshops, and seminars. Be sure to keep your receipts and make a note of what each receipt is for.
- *Equipment Maintenance:* Keep the receipts when you have your equipment worked on.
- *Insurance:* This category can cover everything from general liability to your vehicle insurance. You might want to divide this into a couple of categories depending on how much you pay. Your accountant can give you the IRS's requirements and standards for deductions in this category.
- *Interest:* You can deduct interest paid to company credit cards or any business loans.
- *Legal:* If you have to sue someone for your money or place a lien on a piece of property, or if someone sues you, you will have legal fees. You may also have fees for particular services like writing contracts for a partnership, etc. These are all deductions if they pertain to your business.

- *License and Permits:* This covers contractor's licenses or permits you may have to purchase for jobs.
- *Mailing:* You may not send a lot of packages, but you will be mailing bills. This category covers shipping costs (overnight or otherwise), postage, and even courier services.
- *Office Supplies:* Paper, print cartridges, envelopes, pens, pencils, staplers, and more are covered in this category.
- *Phone Service:* Even if you don't have a business line for your home-based business, you will probably have a cell phone. If the phone is used for business, whether you have just a cell or a cell and an office phone, these expenses can be deducted.
- *Taxes:* This category will include any business tax you pay like business property tax, a percentage of your home's property tax, and any other business tax.
- *Tools:* Items like paintbrushes, putty knives, or paint screens fall under this section. These items should cost under a certain dollar amount each or you will need to depreciate the item over time. Since the amount changes, check with an accountant to see what the current year's amount is.
- *Travel and Lodging:* This can cover a wide range of expenses. Most commonly, it covers expenses incurred when you travel out of town to do a job or attend a seminar or workshop. Keep careful records here. The IRS may want you to prove your expenses were work related.
- *Vehicle Expense:* When you get your oil changed, or new tires, or have your vehicle fixed, you can take the deduction. You can also claim the mileage you drive to and from work.

From the Trenches

Keep your receipts for equipment purchased, food, gas, and paint in a monthly file. When you are justifying your checkbook, haul out these receipts, and check to make sure the numbers you were charged are the ones deducted from your bank account. We once had a paint company take out twice for one purchase.

Depreciating Deductions

These are deductions that cost more than a certain amount of money and are items that the IRS sees as having a life span. You can take deductions on items like computers, ladders, and vehicles, but they must be depreciated, which means that, if you purchase a $1,200 computer, you can deduct a percentage of that amount for the number of years that the IRS views it as a viable piece of business equipment. The depreciating deduction percentage changes from time to time. An accountant will be able to advise you how much of a deduction you can get on your different pieces of equipment.

- *Office Equipment:* This category includes computers, printers, copy machines, or any other office-related equipment.
- *Work Equipment:* Items like airless sprayers, taping machines, and some ladders will fall into this section.
- *Vehicle:* You can deduct your work vehicle over a period of years. Be sure to keep all your purchase papers as your accountant will need to separate the taxes and any fees incurred with the purchase.

Percentage Deductions

You won't be able to take off the total amount of these expenses but instead a percentage according to the size of your office compared with the size of your house. You may think percentage deductions may not help you, but they do add up.

- *Home Office Expense:* You are allowed to take a certain percentage of what it costs for you to operate your office out of your home. You will need to figure out the amount of space you occupy in comparison with the rest of your home. For instance, let's say your home is 2,000 square feet and your office space is 400 square feet. You will be allowed to take off about one-fifth of your house payment. Check with your accountant to get the exact figures.
- *Utilities:* If your home-based business occupies one-fifth of your house, you can typically take one-fifth of your utility bills. Once again check with your accountant.

Keeping Track of What's Coming to You

As you begin working, you will want and need to keep track of who has paid, who needs to pay, and who you need to invoice again. If you have a payment schedule, you need to decide in advance how much you will charge if the client is thirty, sixty, or ninety days late in paying. A good amount is 10 percent per month.

Invoicing

This is the bill you will give your client after you have finished the job. Always give your client a handwritten invoice after every job. You can get generic invoice books at your local office supply store, have them made with your logo printed on them, or make them yourself on your computer. If you get the generic invoice books, purchase a pre-inked stamp so you can stamp your business name and contact information up top for the client. Ideally, the book should have three sheets per invoice. The original will go to the client; you will keep a copy and put the third copy in your client's file. By keeping a copy in your client's file, all you have to do if a question comes up is pull that file, and you will have all the information you need in front of you.

When writing the invoice, besides your business information, include the date, the date the work was performed, the address where the work was performed, a description of the job, and the amount owed. If it is a cost-plus job, you will need to add the cost of materials to the invoice and then separate the hours you worked on the job. A cost-plus job is one where you charge for the cost of the materials and then add the labor hours cost on top of that.

When you get paid for the job, write "paid" on the invoice. If you get paid with a check, it's always a good idea to write the check number on the invoice as well. You might want to add the date you were paid too. To speed the process along, get a pre-inked stamp from your local office supply store that reads "paid." Stamps come in red, black, and blue.

Tips That Make Cents

When you write up your invoice, it is a good idea to add a line at the bottom, "10% added if not paid in 30 days." Some people will pay upon receipt of the invoice, but others will drag it out. Since you completed the job, you shouldn't be out your money. If you don't get paid within thirty days, send another invoice with the 10 percent added. Your creditors would charge you interest and penalty if you didn't pay them.

INVOICE

Your Company Name_____   Client's Name _____

Address_____   Address_____

City, State, Zip _____   City, State, Zip _____

Phone Number _____   Phone Number _____

E-mail Address_____   E-mail Address_____

Date: _____   Job:_____

Job Description_____   Price_____

_____   _____
_____   _____
_____   _____
_____   _____
_____   _____
_____   _____
_____   _____
_____   _____
_____   _____
_____   _____
_____   _____
_____   _____
_____   _____

Total: _____

A Sample Invoice form is included on page 99. An invoice can be as simple or as complex as you choose to make it. When the job is finished, this is what you will give your customer.

Accounts Receivable

Accounts receivable is the amount of money you are owed. If you have a payment plan or you allow thirty days before your client pays you, you will need to keep track of all your outstanding invoices.

An easy way to keep track of these invoices is to get two folders. I prefer the pocket kind. That way invoices won't fall out and get lost. Label one folder "Invoices Due" and keep your outstanding invoices there until they are paid. Label the other folder "Invoices Paid." When an invoice is paid, write or stamp "paid" on it with the date payment was made and move it to the paid folder. If you find an invoice in the "Invoice Due" folder that has been there for thirty days or more, send the client a reminder with a copy of the original invoice. If you haven't been paid after another thirty days, call the client and ask him when you can come by and pick up the amount you are owed.

Invoices Due or Balance

To keep an eye on the bottom line, you need to know how much you are owed on a monthly basis. You can work out a chart that tells you all the information you need to know at a glance. The information on the chart should include the amount you were previously owed, any new invoices you wrote, what deposits you made, and what checks you have on hand that haven't been deposited yet. This should give you a balance of what you are owed. An example chart is found on page 101. A good idea would be to list all the invoices on your chart.

Face the Facts

You should never do a job without having a contract in place, signed and countersigned. Maybe you think you don't need one if you are doing a friend's house. Wrong. There are people out there, friend and foe, who will try to cheat you. It is a fact of life. Realize it early, and you will save yourself a lot of hurt and pain. No matter whose house you are painting, if money is involved, get a contract.

Invoice Balances

Previous Outstanding Invoice Total
    Smith Job ($2,500.00)
    Brown Job ($3,076.00)
    Thomas Job ($1,500.00)
    Watson Job ($1,500.00)
	$8,576.00

New Invoices (2)
    Nickels Job ($2,234.00)
    Cline Job ($2,000.00)
	$4,234.00

Subtotal 1	$12,810.00

Deposits (3)
    Brown Job ($3,076.00)
    Watson Job ($1,500.00)
    Cline Job ($2,000.00)
	$6,576.00

Checks Not Deposited Smith Job ($2,500.00)	$2,500.00
Subtotal 2 (Add deposited checks and checks not deposited.)	$9,076.00
New Outstanding Invoice Total (Subtract Subtotal 2 from Subtotal 1)	$3,734.00

Keeping Track of What You Pay Out

Who Do You Owe and How Much?

Keeping track of who you owe and how much you owe them is just as important as keeping track of who owes you. By keeping your bills up to date and paid, you will be building your business reputation. As with your invoices, an easy way to keep track of your bills is to have two pocket folders. Write on one "Bills Due" and on the other "Bills Paid." Our banker suggested keeping twelve month folders to keep the paid bills in. You might want to move to this system as you get more work and your business grows. For now, two folders should be sufficient.

With that said, you also need a way to keep track of your bills at a glance. The chart on page 103 is how Freedom Painting keeps track of its bills. You can add columns for more description if needed, but your chart should at least contain the following information: date bill is received, bill payable to, amount owed, due date, paid date, amount paid, and check number. Some painters add the address of the biller, and some leave space to include information on what the bill is for. That is up to you. We keep receipts and envelopes so we don't add those two categories.

Petty Cash

Petty cash is the amount of money you take out of your business in cash to spend for your business. You need to keep track of where this money goes as you spend it. Let's say you take out $200.00 and spend $50.00 for gas, $8.00 for lunch, $60.00 for paint, $3.50 for a case of water you take to the job, $10.00 for a clipboard for work purposes, and $2.00 for a pocket calendar. You can make a chart like the one on page 103 that will help you keep track of all these charges. If your petty cash is used for business expenses (and it should be), it is deductible.

General Business Records

When you start a business, there are certain records that you will want and need to keep. These can include everything from a calendar to client records. These can be used to plan your jobs and find work in the future. The following are some records that Freedom Painting keeps on a regular basis. They may or may not work for you. Adapt them so you feel comfortable using them.

Client Files or Folders

When you get a new job, you should first make a client file or folder. Write the client's name or address of the job on the file label. Keep everything pertaining to that job in the file—the bid, paint receipts, and a copy of the final invoice. When you submit the bid, make sure you write down contact information like name, address, phone number, and e-mail address. You never know when you may need this information later.

Job Site Plans and Blueprints

For some jobs, you will get rolls of blueprints; others may consist of two or three copied pages. For those, file them in the appropriate job file. If you receive rolls of blueprints, after the job is bid, put the rolls in an empty paint bucket. Sometimes

Bill Balances

Bill Received On Date	Biller	Amount Owed	Due Date	Paid On	Amount Sent	Check Number
11/5	Sherwin-Williams	$3,050.00	12/1	11/20	$3,050.00	1351
11/8	Anchor	$1,341.00	12/5	11/15	$1,341.00	1343
11/10	Kwal	$6,900.00	12/10			
11/15	Glidden	$678.00	12/15			

Petty Cash Deductions

Date	Item Description	Amount
11/16	Check written for Petty Cash	$200.00
	Expenses	
11/16	Fuel at Conoco	$50.00
11/16	Lunch at Susan's Diner	$8.00
11/16	Paint—Sherwin-Williams for Smith Job	$60.00
11/16	Discount Store—Case of Water	$3.50
11/16	Discount Store—Clipboard	$10.00
11/16	Discount Store—Pocket Calculator	$2.00
11/16	Expense Subtotal	$133.50
11/16	Petty Cash Left	$66.50

your clients will want them back at the end of the job. If they don't request them back, keep them for six months before you dispose of them. David has had to refer to blueprints several times over the course of a job.

Today, most jobs are sent via e-mail. Painters can open blueprints or plans on their computer screen and bid jobs from there. Make files for each of these blueprints and give them the same name as on your physical folders. If you decide to bid, give estimates, and send invoices electronically, make sure you back up everything and keep separate files for different jobs just as you would physically.

Appointment Book

An appointment book and an organizer will be your saving grace. When you start working, it is difficult to keep track of everything going on around you. With an appointment book, you can write down where you are supposed to be on which days and what time you are expected there. If you are to meet with another client or contractor, write it in your book. I always have David look at his the night before, just in case he needs to send his crew to a job before he arrives because he has another appointment.

Some organizers have calendars in them and day-to-day space or week-at-a-glance space where you can write down what you need to do on any given day. Your "To Do" list needs to stay current, and make it a rule to not mark off your tasks until they are done. We have used a two-page-spread-per-day organizer for years. It gets us to our appointments on time and gets jobs completed. I feel these types of books are essential for any business owner. It may take you several trials over a couple of years to find one you are comfortable with, but definitely get one and use it.

Address Book

A Rolodex or address book is needed to help you keep in touch with all your clients and contacts. Whichever you buy, I would suggest getting one with plastic sleeves to slip business cards in. You will no doubt be given business cards from contractors, paint reps, other subcontractors like drywall workers or paperhangers, and maybe from your clients. Having these plastic sleeves to hold business cards will save you a lot of time, headache, and worry. By having these in a safe place, you will be able to get in touch with people when you need them. The ideal situation would be to have your contacts on a device or in a book you can take with you when you leave your office. You never know when you will need to call a client, and if someone isn't home to get a number for you, you could lose an opportunity.

When you get a new client, you should first enter his address, phone number, and e-mail in your address book. You will be building a database to send out flyers or contact them about future jobs.

Of course, if you are doing all of your work electronically, you can set up a system so that when you enter the contact information on your estimate or bid sheets, it automatically goes into a database. Check around for computer and phone sync-able apps. These may take a while to learn but will save you time in the long run.

Forms

As you start out and then as your business grows, you will need certain types of forms and charts. Some are standard, and some you can wait on and use as needed. The bid or estimate sheet, invoice (discussed earlier in the chapter), mileage chart, and to-do list are probably the most basic and most used forms. You will want to make them standard on all your jobs. You can create them on your computer or buy them from your local office supply store.

Most of these forms will keep you organized, but some will be needed as a record for the Internal Revenue Service and some are required by law. Just as permits and licenses vary from state to state, legal paper requirements do so too, so be sure to check with your state to see what you need.

As your business grows, you may want to think about putting together a short form letter or basic e-mail that tells potential clients what you do and your average price. These e-mails or letters will have the advantage of providing a personal touch without your having to reinvent your work expertise every time someone contacts you.

Over the next several pages are some forms and general ideas for helping with the management of your business. Pick and choose what works for you and what is needed for your state's requirements. Feel free to modify any of the forms to your needs.

Bid or Estimate Sheet

On the bid or estimate sheet, you will include a place for your name and contact information and your client's name and contact information. There should also be a place for the address of the job. Be sure to include the date the bid was given, a description of the job you will perform, the price, as well as anything you need your client to do like moving furniture out of the way. You should also have a place for the client to sign or "okay" the estimate. An okay is just good business sense. It protects you and your client.

To bid an existing ceiling and wall job, you will need to take some measurements. Take your tape measure and measure the length of the walls. Let's say you have two walls at ten feet each (twenty feet) and another two at fifteen feet each (thirty feet). The height of the walls is eight feet. Multiply the wall length (fifty) and the height (eight), and you will have your square footage (four hundred square feet). To get the square footage of the ceiling, multiply the length of one wall (ten feet) and the length of the other (fifteen feet). In this case, it will be 150 square feet. Now add the wall square footage (400) with the ceiling square footage (150) and you will have 550. An average bid is around $1 a square foot for labor. The ceiling will need only one coat of paint while the walls will need two coats. Since a gallon of paint covers about three hundred square feet, you will need about three gallons of paint at $20 each, or $60. Your final bid will be $550 (550 square feet x $1 a square foot) plus the $60 cost of the paint (three gallons at $20), or $610. Most painters will round that amount down to $600.

The Sample Estimate Worksheet on page 107 will help you figure out a bid, and an example of a bid or estimate sheet can be found on page 108.

Mileage Chart

When you drive your business vehicle to and from jobs, you need to keep track of how many miles you've driven, how much gas you've purchased, your tire pressure, and notes about any repairs that might be needed or have been made, like an oil change. You will need to keep these charts so you can prove your mileage to the Internal Revenue Service when tax time rolls around.

The Sample Mileage Chart on page 109 can be used for a week and will take up only half a regular size sheet of paper. So you can include two to a page and use the back of the sheet and have an entire month on one sheet.

ESTIMATE WORKSHEET

Job: _____Date:_____

1) Measurement of length of walls (measure in feet):

    Wall 1)_____

    Wall 2)_____

    Wall 3)_____

    Wall 4)_____

Total of four walls: _____

2) Height of wall: _____

3) Multiply total wall length and wall height = square footage.

    _____ x _____=_____

(Note: If you are only doing the walls, skip the ceiling square footage.)

4) Ceiling Square Footage

    Multiply the length of one wall and the length of the wall next to it = ceiling square footage.

    _____ x _____ = _____

5) Add total wall square footage + ceiling square footage = total square footage.

    _____ + _____ = _____

6) Multiply the square footage by how much you are going to charge for labor.

    _____ x $_____ = $ _____

7) Divide total square footage by 300 = number of gallons of paint you will need. Multiply that number by two because you will probably have to put two coats on the walls. Then multiply that number by how much your paint cost per gallon. This will give you the paint cost.

    _____ ÷ 300 = _____ x 2 = _____ x $_____ = $ _____

8) Add the total in 6 plus the total in 7. This will give you the total estimate.

    $_____ + $ _____ = $_____

ESTIMATE

Your Company Name_____   Client's Name _____

Address_____   Address_____

City, State, Zip _____   City, State, Zip _____

Phone Number _____   Phone Number_____

E-mail Address_____   E-mail Address_____

Date: _____   Job:_____

Job Description_____   Price_____

_____   _____

_____   _____

_____   _____

_____   _____

_____   _____

_____   _____

Comments: (Write here what you will do or what the client needs to do, like move furniture away from the walls, etc.)

_____

_____

_____

_____

_____

I accept and approve this estimate. Date: _____

Signature: _____

_____

MILEAGE CHART

Vehicle Driven: _____   Week: _____

Oil Change Date:_____   Mileage at Oil Change: _____

	Mon.	Tues.	Wed.	Thurs.	Fri.	Sat.	Sun.	Total
Beginning Mileage								
Ending Mileage								
Miles Driven								
Amount Spent On Gas								
Gallons Used								
Turnpike Fees								
Other								

Notes: _____

_____

_____

_____

_____

EQUIPMENT MAINTENANCE LOG

Equipment:_____

Date	Job Site	Hours Used	Employee	How Ran?

Comments: _____

_____

_____

Equipment Maintenance Log

You probably won't need this form right away, but as you grow and have employees using your equipment, you will want to keep track of who is using the equipment, how long it was used, on which job, and when it was last serviced.

Equipment and Paint Log

At some point, you will need to know what equipment you own, how much you paid for it, and when you bought it. This will come in handy not only for reporting to the IRS, but also for buying insurance or proving to law enforcement that you actually owned the equipment if, heaven forbid, you are ever robbed. By keeping a log of the paint on hand, you can determine easily if you can use what you have on a job or if the paint is old, and needs to be disposed of. Paint can last anywhere from six months to four years depending on what kind of paint it is, if the paint has been opened, or how many times the paint can has been opened, which can cause certain kinds of paint to dry out quickly. Each type of paint is different.

EQUIPMENT AND PAINT LOG

Equipment Name	Serial No. or How Many	Date Purchased	Where Purchased	Cost	Date Serviced	What Was Done

06

Building Your Team

In this chapter, we will look at your internal and external teams, where to find them, how to choose them, when they are needed, and what they can do for you. If you build a strong team, your business will prosper and grow. If you choose a weak one, you can have untold headaches and your business could collapse.

Consider your internal team the backbone of your business or your support personnel. Some you will pay; others will just work with you. Each one is important and needs to be carefully chosen as he or she can be the difference between success and failure.

Your external team will be those who work with you on the job every day. They will be the ones other people see and the ones who talk and interact with your clients. They will be your workforce, also known as your employees.

Now, let's get to work at looking at each of your teams.

Your Internal Team

No matter whom you decide to work with, make sure you check them out thoroughly. Remember, not only do they need to be affordable and capable, but they also need to have your business's best interest at heart, be around for the long haul, have integrity, and be trustworthy. Do not rush into any decision on these people. Interview them as you would a business partner because that is basically what these people will wind up being. Take your time. Talk to others who work with them and get their opinions. People already in business suggest that you look at the following five areas when considering your internal team: accessibility, compatibility, ethics, price, and qualifications:

- *Accessibility:* Most professionals are always busy, but make sure the people you are considering are not so overcommitted that they can't talk to you when you need them the most. There will be times when you will be in a pinch and need to talk to someone *now*. If the professional can't get around to you for a week or more, what good will he do you? If a professional keeps putting you off, look for someone else.

■ *Compatibility:* Can you talk freely to this person? Do you have an easy rapport? Does he listen to what you are saying, and does he take your business as seriously as you do? Does he know anything about home-based businesses and construction? When looking at a professional, you want to make sure he or she has knowledge in these two areas. If you work with an attorney who has never sued or protected construction interests, he won't know everything that can happen along the way, perhaps leaving you in a tidal wave of litigation you are unprepared for.

■ *Ethics:* Is the person you are considering honest? Does he have integrity? Does he have the same ethical standards you have? When he tells you something, does he stick to it? Working with someone who is always changing his mind, works in gray areas, or fudges on deals can be a problem later on.

■ *Price:* What will you be charged? While you shouldn't choose a professional based on his price alone, you do still want to be diligent with your dollars. By checking into a professional's qualifications, experience, and skills, and then comparing prices, you should be able to find a competent and affordable professional.

■ *Qualifications:* What qualifications does this person have to do the job you need him to do? Look at the person's background. What prepared him for his position? How long has he been in this type of business? Where did he learn his business? You don't want to work with someone who plays around in his area of expertise or does it part time. We have heard of many people who have run into major problems because they went to a part-time accountant to have their taxes done because he was a friend of a friend, did people's taxes in the spring as a side job to make extra money, and charged less than a certified public accountant (CPA). The end result was always disastrous because the part-time accountant wasn't up on the latest tax laws and wasn't available when problems like audits arose. Find a professional who is as dedicated to his business as you are to yours.

Think about all these suggestions before you hire any professionals. Remember, they can either help or hurt your business.

Who Should You Work With

In the next section, we will look at specific professionals the house painter can go to for help and support.

Banker

The first person you will want to build a relationship with is your banker. He will be the one you can go to when you consider expanding your business, need a loan, or have to get a check approved right away to make payroll or pay your bills. A banker can set up a line of credit for you and warn you if it looks as if you may be getting in over your head. Bankers typically have their fingers on the pulse of the community and know about local trends—highs and lows.

We have had the same banker for more than thirty years. In fact, when she moved from bank to bank, we moved with her because she knew our business and us. She has given us loans to buy new vehicles and help expand our business, and has directed us to collection companies when we needed to get payment from a contractor. Because bankers are working in a community-based environment, they typically know the local people who can help you and your business. They stay on top of what's going on not only in the financial world, i.e., the stock market, but in the community as well.

Our banker, Jane Haskin, recommended that anyone wanting to start a business should make an appointment to talk to his banker. "Sit down and tell him what you had in mind for your business," Haskin said. "He can direct you which way to go financially with banking accounts, saving accounts, retirement funds, and more." The banker may even be able to direct you to an insurance agent if you don't have one for your business needs.

It really doesn't matter which bank you choose as long as you can work with its staff and its staff is willing to work with you. Our bank is a small neighborhood bank; we like the one-on-one personal service. Larger banks may be able to offer you more services, like a revolving business line of credit, bigger loans, and business credit cards. Remember, though, that with more services, you may be charged higher fees, so be cautious and thorough when looking for a bank.

Accountant

You may not need an accountant at first, but eventually you will. You may just need an accountant to figure out your yearly taxes, and we strongly recommend you find one to do that. Besides doing your income taxes, though, an accountant can help you with tax planning, monthly statements, profit and loss statements, taking care of audits whether from your insurance company or the IRS, and tax issues and problems, plus they can advise you on which purchases would be beneficial for your company by way of tax deductions.

We have worked with the same accounting firm for more than thirty years and are on our third accountant, not because we didn't like the accountants but because the previous accountants passed away. So you could say that Freedom Painting has outlived our accountants. Our current accountant, Hazel Boone, has worked with us for fifteen years. She is a certified public accountant (CPA) and costs a little more, but is well worth the price.

A CPA is the best way to go if you can afford it. CPAs have met their state's educational requirements and have college degrees, have passed a certification test, and have ongoing annual education requirements.

Boone figures our monthly books, does monthly and year-end statements, does our income taxes, and handles all our audits. We typically get audited once or twice a year by the insurance company that carries our workers' compensation insurance. She has also gone to battle for us with the Internal Revenue Service when it informed us that we owed an additional $5,000 for some tax. In the end, we found that the IRS had combined another company's taxes from another state that had a similar name as ours. We didn't owe any money, and after about eight months, she finally got the problem worked out with the IRS.

When choosing an accountant, make sure that she or he is qualified. Does he have experience working with home-based businesses? Is he familiar with your business, its ups and downs? Does he attend seminars at least every other year to learn the new tax laws and the changes that will impact you and your business taxes? Be sure to investigate your accountant thoroughly. Ask him if he takes care of audits? How many home-based business clients does he have? How long has he been in business? Where and how is he certified?

Insurance Agent

If possible, find an agent who can handle *all* your business insurance needs. You will need insurance for your vehicles, property insurance, health insurance, workers' comp, etc. Most agents will work for one agency but have access to several companies that can provide different types of insurance.

As in all of your other decisions, take time in choosing your insurance agent. Ask around and get references from others in the construction trade. After you get some names, get three or four bids from several agencies on the different kinds of insurance you might need. Look at the coverage each agency offers and compare the quotes each gives. You will want the best coverage for the price you will pay. Find out the qualifications and experience level of the agent you will be working with and take the time to speak with the agent face to face. Ask him if he has experience working with home-based businesses and if he knows about your type of business— painting. Find out if he is familiar with bonds. You want to find an agent who will not undersell you a policy nor oversell. If he oversells, you will be paying too high of a premium for the coverage you are receiving. If he undersells, you might not have the coverage you need should the unthinkable happen.

Like our banker and accountant, we have had the same insurance agent for many years. We appreciate the way she keeps in touch with us, and when premiums are raised on our policies, she always investigates new companies and notifies us of alternative pricing. She knows our business, how many vehicles we carry, the workers' comp load we need, as well as our bonding requirements and obligations.

Attorney

Finding an attorney can be intimidating. Attorneys charge a lot of money and are typically not the easiest people to get along with, but when you need one, you need one. The best way to find an attorney is to ask around in the construction business for referrals. You will want an attorney who specializes in business and knows the construction trade. Do an interview over the phone or schedule a meeting in person. Most business attorneys will not charge an initial meeting fee. If they do charge, look for someone else. Interview the attorney as you would a business partner. Make a list of questions and ask them.

There are a number of areas in which an attorney can assist you: They can help you with the correct legal structure for your business and complete the papers, write up a partnership agreement, write up employment papers for your employees, represent you in court if you are sued or if you need to sue, write a will, and in the worst-case scenario, help you with bankruptcy.

As an alternative to an attorney, you can work with a paralegal. Paralegals are cheaper than attorneys and can advise you when you might need an attorney. The services most paralegals can provide is limited, but you would be surprised at what they can do at one-fourth of the price of an attorney. Our paralegal files all of our liens. When we needed to sue a contractor, she gave us the name of an attorney. When we contacted the attorney, we were surprised that he had sued this company in the past and was in the middle of suing it again on behalf of plumbers and electricians. He added us to the list.

Product Sales Reps

You should get to know the people you will be buying your paint, paint supplies, and paint equipment from. They work at the stores you will be frequenting and are typically the managers of the stores. After you get to know these reps, they will typically give you the best prices they have available. They can help you find colors, mix paint for special tints, give you quotes, get your paint to the job site, and help with your account if a problem arises.

Don't be hesitant about meeting and talking to these guys. You are one of the people who keep them in business, so they should take the time to talk to you and be more than happy to do it.

If possible, meet with the regional manager of the paint stores as well. If you have problems with a local store, he can go over the local manager's head and take care of your problem.

David was to start a big job in a different town from where he normally worked, and he needed a specific type of fire-retardant paint. For some reason the local paint store kept stalling, telling him it couldn't get the paint he needed. When the day arrived for him to need this paint and the paint store still didn't have it, he called the regional manager. The regional manager got the paint and had it to David, on the job site, in twenty-four hours.

There may be other internal personnel you need to find as your business grows, but these basic five will get you started and should be the least you start with. Even if you don't need an accountant or an attorney right away, start asking around to get an idea of whom you will want to contact when you need them. It's always best to follow the Boy Scout motto, "Be Prepared."

Your External Team

Now it's time to look at building your external team. At first, your external team may just be you, but if you want to expand your business, you will eventually want and need to hire employees. How many and for how long is up to you. Freedom Painting has employed as few as two and as many as twelve at any given time. The construction business ebbs and flows. Sometimes you will have a lot of work and at other times barely enough to keep yourself busy.

Remember, as we look into this, the more employees you hire, the more money they will cost you. That's just part of the business. However, having employees will also allow you to pick up more jobs, thus making more money. You must remember, too, that if you decide to hire full-time employees, you need to get and retain enough work to keep everyone busy.

From the start you needed to have an internal team working for you and you picked them carefully to make sure they were the right fit for you. Now you need to

Around the Paint Bucket

If you don't have any external team members yet, ask people in the construction business for recommendations. Word travels fast, and you can quickly learn who you should work with and who you should stay away from.

think, consider, and pick your external team, your employees, just as carefully. Hire the right employees, and they will work and make you money. Choose the wrong employees, and you will wind up spending all your time fixing the messes they made and losing money.

Employees

Let's start off by looking at employees (full time and part time) versus subcontractors (or subs).

Full-Time Employees

These employees are the ones who come to the job every day. They are the ones who will keep your business up and running. The advantage to having full-time employees is that you know someone will be on the job whether you are running behind because of a meeting or you have to leave to bid another job. The downside is that if you have full-time employees, you need to have enough work to keep them busy. You don't want to let full-time employees go if you have trained them and they are hard and honest workers. You don't want to have to start from scratch.

Part-Time Employees

These employees are just that, part time. They are the ones who come and go as work comes and goes. Spring, especially summer, and fall are typically construction's busiest times. You may want to hire two or three extra people to help during this period.

Be up front with your part-time employees. Let them know that this is only temporary employment. Most will know and not care as long as they have work for a while. Keep your temporary help's contact information in case you need them during the off-season or you have picked up an extra job. Sometimes part-time employees move on and find other jobs, which can be a pain for you because you have to train new part-time employees all over again.

A good pool to draw from for part-time employees is college students and school teachers. They are out of school over the summer and are typically looking for things to do. Remember, though, that the same rights like breaks, safety issues, and discrimination laws, apply to part-time employees as they do to full-time employees.

Subcontractors

Subcontractors are an additional workforce for your company without all the hassles of employees. Subcontractors, or subs, work for you after you have a job. Subs typically have their own business and come in to complete a task that you hire them for. For instance, let's say you have a house to paint and you have two accent or art walls to do. You hire a subcontractor who is an expert in accent walls. It's still your job, but someone else is taking over part of it.

You will want to get a bid from the sub and add it to the cost of your original bid with a percentage added on for you. When you are paid, you will pay the sub his bid and keep the rest for yourself.

The advantage to having a subcontractor is that he has his own business, so you don't have to worry about taxes, insurance, workers' comp, etc. The sub is already trained, has his own equipment, pays his own expenses, and is responsible for his own work. The downside is that a sub sets his own hours, works on his own terms, and cannot be fired like an employee can.

Typically subs are hard workers as they are just as determined to build their businesses as you are yours. When looking for subcontractors, check around to see what kind of work they do, if they are reliable, and if they have integrity.

Freedom Painting has a paperhanger who works as a sub. About eight years ago, besides painting, Freedom also hung wallpaper and different types of wall coverings. We were painting hotels, and the owners wanted their lobbies covered with paper. To keep up with the jobs we bid, we had to hire a sub to hang the paper. He now does all our paper work. David bids the wallpaper in with the regular bid, and then he hires Danny to do the work.

Who's Running the Job

If you hire employees, part time or full time, you need to make clear who is running the job from the start. You may be on the job site if you are running a small crew and have one job. However, if you have to leave a job site and your workers or you have several jobs and have to split up your crews, you will need to leave someone in charge.

Ideally, you will choose someone who has been working with you longer than anyone else. Besides longevity, the person in charge should have three other qualities:

- *Is this person responsible?* You need to put someone in charge who will keep the crew working. If this person is going to let the crew go home before a full day's work is complete or start fooling around the minute you walk out the door, he could be putting not only your reputation, but your business, in jeopardy.
- *Does this person have painting experience?* You need to leave someone in charge who knows how to paint and also take care of any problems or questions that come up from the crew while they are painting. If you leave someone in charge who is not experienced, you may come back to a disaster or an unfinished job.
- *Does this person have people skills?* Don't put a hothead or someone who doesn't get along with others on the job in charge of them. The crew members don't all have to like your supervisor, but they do have to respect him. Does he have a positive attitude? Can he motivate your crew to work while you are gone? If a problem does come up among your crew, can he settle disputes peacefully?

You don't always have to have a supervisor, but if you are not there, someone needs to be in charge. Take your time in choosing that person because he can become your biggest help or your biggest hindrance.

Where to Find Employees

The next job you face is finding your employees and making sure they are ready and willing to work. You will want people who are dependable, so you don't have to worry about whether they will show up on the job from morning to morning. You will also want someone who is willing to work and not just expect to get paid because he shows up. We'll talk about screening your applicants a little later; for now let's just find some warm bodies.

- *Ads in Newspapers:* All newspapers have a classified section and in that section is "Help Wanted" or "Employment." You can run a small ad ranging in price from $20 to $300 a month depending on the size and circulation of the newspaper. You don't have to say much. "Need Qualified Painters, Call 314-555-1212" will work. You can also post your information online with Craigslist (www.craigslist.com) under the Jobs category for your area.

- *Friends and Relatives:* Sometimes this group of people will know someone who needs work. A word of caution, don't put someone to work just because he is your friend or relative. Treat him as you would an employee from the start. Let the person know right off the bat that, when he is on the job, you are not his friend or relative, but his boss. He will respect you for it later.

- *Contractors:* Contractors move from job to job like you do. They may know of a painter from another job whose work is currently slow. This can be a quick and temporary fix if you get in a bind. Ask what kind of job this person does, if he's reliable, and if the contractor would work with him again. If so, contact that person and put him to work.

- *Paint Store:* When painters are looking for work, they typically tell people at the paint store and leave their cards there. The paint store will usually know how successful they have been in the past by the amount of paint they have purchased. Pick up a couple of cards and keep them in your files for future reference.

- *Bulletin Boards:* You can make signs or flyers requesting what kind of work you need help for and leave them on community bulletin boards. Most home supply and paint stores have bulletin boards as do junior, technical, and four-year colleges.

What You Need to Know

Now that you have decided to hire some employees, there are some rules and regulations you should know. There are certain things an employer can and cannot do, as set forth by the United States Department of Labor. We will discuss some of them here, but you can get current information by visiting the department's website at www.dol.gov. An employee's rights and government regulations change all the time. Make sure you have updated information for your business. The government doesn't care that you may not know.

Minimum Wage

You must at least pay your employees minimum wage. You could start the people you need to train at minimum wage but pay your experienced employees a higher wage. Even if you are using an intern, you must pay him something. The government doesn't allow free labor on job sites. If someone works, that person gets paid. Period. As of July 2009, the federal minimum wage rate was $7.25 an hour. However, be aware that some states and municipalities have a higher minimum wage than the federal's and the higher minimum wage applies.

Working Hours

The government standard workweek is forty hours a week or eight hours a day. This typically can be a work schedule of 8:00 a.m. to 10:15 a.m. and then a fifteen-minute break. Back to work at 10:30 a.m. until noon and then another break for a thirty-minute lunch. Employees will go back to work from 12:30 p.m. until 2:30 p.m. at which time they will have another fifteen-minute break and then work until 5:00 p.m.

Overtime

If your employees work more than forty hours a week, you must pay overtime. That consists of time and a half of their normal scheduled salary. For instance, if you pay an employee $15 an hour, you would need to pay him $22.50 (his usual $15 plus $7.50) an hour beginning the forty-first hour he worked.

Child Labor Laws

The Fair Labor Standards Act states that an employer can't employ anyone under the age of fourteen and any minor under sixteen can only work a limited number of hours. There are also job-safety requirements for minors under the age of eighteen

that limit the types of jobs they can do at work sites. States carry different rules
and regulations about child labor, so check with your state department of labor
for compliance.

Required Garnishments

It probably won't happen a lot, but there may be instances when you have to take
funds out of an employee's base pay to give to the IRS for back taxes or to the state
for back child support. State or federal officials will tell you where to send the money.
This may create a little more paperwork for you, but *you* will need to do it. Don't give
your employee his full wages and expect him to do it. If he hasn't paid these bills yet,
he probably won't, and then you will be left paying them in addition to his wages.

Discrimination

The federal government in the Civil Rights Act of 1964 prohibits you from discrimi-
nating against anyone you may hire, promote, discharge, pay, give benefits to, train,
refer, or any other aspects of employment on the basis of race, gender, color, religion,
national origin, age, smoking habits, or physical handicaps (unless those handicaps
prevent the person from doing the job). As time has gone by, other discriminatory
taboos have been added to the list: weight, sexual orientation, marital status, and
pregnancy. These laws are changing all the time, and your state or local govern-
ments may have regulations of their own. Be sure to check not only with the U.S.
Department of Labor, but your state's labor department as well.

Sexual Harassment

The Equal Employment Opportunity Commission defines sexual harassment as
"unwelcome sexual advances, requests for sexual favors, and other verbal or

physical conduct of a sexual nature." The U.S. Supreme Court has defined two kinds of sexual harassment. One type is when the action or nonaction (sexual favors) affects employment status, like being fired, demoted, or passed over for promotion. The second is referred to as working in a hostile environment. A hostile environment can be defined as one where there is discussion of sexual activities, the telling of off-color jokes, unwanted and unnecessary touching, commenting on physical attributes, the use of indecent gestures, and the use of crude and offensive language, to name a few examples. Not only do you need to be aware of these issues, but so do your employees. Be up front with them, and let them know that harassment will not be tolerated. Letting them know your expectations right away will save you headaches down the road.

Workplace Safety

While we will discuss workplace safety more in depth in the next chapter, you need to know that, if a workplace accident involving injury or death happens, it needs to be reported to the Occupational Safety and Health Administration (OSHA) within eight hours of the incident. You are responsible for the safety of your workers on the job, and OSHA is clear about how a construction site must be manned, like wearing hard hats and/or using respirators. Visit OSHA's website at www.osha.gov to not only read accident reports, but also review the agency's regulations.

Drug Tests

Today, with the need for complete safety on the job site, employers are allowed to make their employees take a drug test. Typically the drugs being tested for are illicit drugs like marijuana, crack, PCP, heroin, and other harmful substances. As an employer, you can get these tests conducted at hospitals or clinics and do them randomly or as a condition of employment. The best way to handle these tests is to tell your employees that drugs and alcohol won't be tolerated. Educate them as to the harmful effects of drugs and alcohol and have a plan in place if one of your employees tests positive.

Background and Credit Checks

Employers are legally allowed to run background and credit checks on those they are considering hiring. There are limitations to what information can be requested, however, and you must inform the prospective employee of the credit check. Most employers wait until they are down to the final steps of the hiring process before running a background check, because these checks cost money. You may not feel that running checks is necessary, but if you do, the option is available to you.

As you work more with employees, you will find further practices and regulations you need to know. These are just the basics. Continue to investigate and check out the government's rules and standards to stay on top of what you need to know.

What Your Employees Need to Know

Now, just as you need to know certain rules and regulations, there is information you need to tell your employees, such as what you expect from them, how they are to conduct themselves on the job site, pay, hours, and other items relevant to them. While talking face to face is always a good idea, it is also prudent to write down the information so that the employee can refer to it if any questions arise. This protects you in case the employee says he didn't know about a certain policy.

To make sure your employee has all the information he needs, you have to write a company manual. Writing a company manual isn't difficult. Think about what you want in an employee and what you will not condone, and then write it all down. Consider your company manual your business policy. Here are some guidelines and areas that should be addressed when you write your manual.

Company Manual

When writing your company manual, you should include certain key elements like detailed information about your business's policies and expectations for employees. These should include the following topics: attendance, tardy policies and excused absences, dress code, safety policies, drugs and alcohol, and any legal information your employee needs to know, like sexual harassment information.

For each of these items, you also need to include what action will be taken against the employee if your company's policies aren't followed. Be clear, so that any employee can understand the information. If you decide to have zero tolerance in any of these areas, spell that out explicitly. You also want to make sure that there are no statements that contradict one another so employees can't find a loophole in your policies.

It is always a good idea to have an attorney look at your company manual. He can guide you in language that needs to be changed, items that are unclear, or issues that may cause problems later on.

Start your manual by writing a little bit about your business. Tell your employee who you are, why and when you started painting. You might include your business statement, your business goals, and what opportunities are available to your employees, if any. From there move to the particulars.

Attendance, Tardy Policy, and Excused Absences
Most employers carry a "zero tolerance" policy when it comes to attendance. However, there are days when employees catch flu bugs and will have a variety of illnesses. You need to decide how many sick days you will allow your employees and how far in advance they need to notify you if they are not going to be at work.

Next decide on what will be excused absences. Obviously, if your employee is vomiting or running to the bathroom every five minutes, his work is going to be hindered. While that may be excused, a runny nose or spring fever will not be. Most employers request a doctor's note. The general thought is that, if one is sick enough to stay home from work, one should go to the doctor. Of course, there are times when you don't want your employees at work, like if they have H1N1 or hepatitis. While this may be an excused absence, it doesn't mean they will continue to get paid unless you have a number of "excused absences with pay" written into your manual.

There are occasions when your employees may get stuck in traffic. Five minutes late can be a red light or the employee's clock may be off by five minutes. Beyond that, start deducting pay, or at the very least keep track. If you follow a "zero tolerance" policy on late arrival, tell your employees and stick to it. Let the employee figure out how early he has to leave for work to arrive on time. You are not a babysitter or your employee's father. If he overslept, make it a policy that he calls you and lets you know he is going to be late. You will also need to address the chronically late person. A good rule to follow is to pull him aside and address the issue, offering a second chance. After that, if the infraction continues, you may have to let the person go. Allowing one person to get away with something will breed contempt among the rest of your employees.

Dress Code
Here you will need to address what is acceptable and what is not regarding dress on the work site. While painters wear white, you may not care if your employees wear jeans and T-shirts. State that in your policy. You need to decide if shorts and tank

tops will be tolerated. While you may be flexible on clothing, you might want to walk a hard line on lip and nose piercings. These may cause a health hazard on the job, not to mention a perception of a lack of professionalism.

One absolute is the wearing of solid shoes—no open-toed shoes or sandals on the job. Many construction workers have lost toes or tripped over equipment or door jambs and been injured because they wore inappropriate shoes. You don't want to lose a valuable employee, be sued for work injuries, or have the government come down on you for preventable workplace safety issues.

Make sure you consider all these ideas and put them in writing. That way your employees can't come back to you and say they didn't know.

Safety Policies

On any job site, there will be certain risks to your employees. Your job is to minimize those risks by educating them in safety or at the very least giving them a set of guidelines to follow on the job. For instance, some jobs will require hard hats. Insist your employees wear them. If employees need to climb ladders, make sure they have a spotter or are tied off. If there are spills, these are to be cleaned up immediately to keep employees from slipping and falling. Another safety hazard for painters is electrocution. We will discuss this issue more in depth in the next chapter, but for the manual make sure your employees are aware how to check for "hot boxes" and use the proper equipment around electrical lines.

Substance Abuse

This should definitely be a "zero tolerance" area. Of course, your employees should be allowed to take prescribed pharmaceuticals and over-the-counter remedies, but alcohol and illicit drugs should not be tolerated. There is too much of a risk of harm to not only the employee using, but to other employees and the job site itself. Make it clear at the very beginning that if any employee brings drugs or alcohol to the premises or if they are drunk or high when they arrive or anytime during the day, it is immediate grounds for dismissal. Period.

If an employee does arrive at the work site impaired and you send that person home, take that person home yourself or make another employee take him home. If he arrives at work and you know he is impaired, you may be culpable if he gets into an accident after you sent him home.

Legal Issues

Employers are always faced with legal issues like the one mentioned above. However, the biggest issue on the work site today is sexual harassment.

Since sexual harassment is such a big issue, make sure that you are clear about what you expect from your employees. In your manual, you can include the Department of Labor's definition of sexual harassment and what actions encompass sexual harassment. Be specific and make sure your employees understand what a serious issue this can become. You don't want to be run off a job or sued because of something one of your employees did.

Hiring

You've gotten the word out that you need employees and defined how you would like them to act on the job. Now it's time to do some actual hiring. While you may have many applicants, choose and hire only the ones who show promise and look as if they will be a benefit to your business. In some instances, you will have to be tough. Don't fall for the sob story and hire someone because "he is down on his luck." You are looking for hard workers. You are not running a charity house.

What to Pay

Deciding what to pay can be problematic. Keep in mind, however, that while you do have to pay minimum wage, you don't have to pay top dollar if someone has never painted before and you are training him. You should look at it as, the more valuable to the business and skilled the employee is, the more he gets paid. Another factor in deciding pay is whether the person works well on his own or has to be constantly supervised.

Applications

This is your first defense in finding out who will be good for your business and who definitely won't. There are certain questions you will want to ask on your application and certain questions you can't ask because of privacy issues and government standards. The best way to go is to purchase application forms from your local office supply store. These will typically have all the information you need, but double-check to make sure the applicant will be giving you his contact information, driver's license number, Social Security number, education, work history, and references.

Have your prospective employee turn in his application at least a week before you interview him. There are specific items you will want to review. His driver's license number will allow you to check his driving record, especially if he will be driving a company vehicle. Getting his Social Security number will save you loads of time when tax time rolls around or when your accountant or insurance agent needs it.

Look at his employment record. Has he worked at one or two jobs or is he working for a different company every six months? Has he moved up in these companies? How long has he been unemployed? What types of jobs has he had? As far as his education, if he has written down that he has a college degree, how is his spelling, grammar, and punctuation? People who have a college degree typically have taken some basic English classes. While this may not be a big deal to you, it's more to judge a person's integrity than anything else. If someone will lie on his application, can you trust him on the job?

Don't neglect to check references and check all the references given, not just the applicant's last employer. You may think you don't have time, but this would be a major mistake. You will want to verify the information he put on his application with his past employers. You need to know why this person was let go or why he quit. What were his duties? What kind of work did he do? How did he get along with others? If he didn't get along with others, what were some of the problems? How was his attendance at work? Did the employer ever have any trouble with him? Was he a valued member of his employer's team? Other questions may come to mind as you are reviewing the applications. Be sure to write them down as they come to you and don't hesitate to ask them.

If a person requests that you not contact his current employer, respect his wishes, but make it a point to ask why he doesn't want you contacting him. One employee we had was afraid that, if we contacted the person he was working for at the time of the interview, he would be let go immediately on his other job. He had seen it happen to fellow employees. He needed the job, so he didn't want his present employer to know he was looking at other options.

The Interview

Now is the time to get all the questions answered that came up as you looked over your prospective employee's application, plus straighten out any discrepancies you may have noticed. There may be a simple explanation if he wrote that it took him five years to finish high school. Maybe he had an illness that took him out of school for a year. Schedule a time when you are not hurried and can respond to any questions your interviewee may have as well.

Beyond what was on the application, you may want to ask some of these questions: Why did you leave or why do you want to leave your current employer? Why do you want to work for my company? What do you hope to gain by coming to work for my company?

If this is his first job, ask why he wants to work in the construction trade, specifically house painting. What does he think he can do to benefit the business? Is he willing to be trained and do a lot of grunt work until he can be promoted? One of our most valued employees was fresh out of high school. He worked for Freedom Painting for years until he became ill and lost his eyesight. We still keep in touch with him and are glad to report that he is doing well in his new computer job.

Some applicants may seem nervous. Some may seem evasive. The purpose of the interview is to get to know the person you are about to employ. If you feel uncomfortable, if you are not getting straight answers, or if your personalities don't click, don't hire this person. As a matter of fact, it makes good sense to make no promises on the day of the interview. Thank the person for coming in and then tell him you'll be in touch in a few days. That will give you some time to think about the interviews, do background searches on viable candidates, and gather more information if you need to.

Don't feel guilty about hiring a few and not the rest. It may sound cruel, but your job is not to save the world but to hire people who will work for you and help build your business. Don't make it personal. It's business and that's all.

When doing interviews, schedule them at a restaurant, library, coffee shop, or some other public place. You don't want to invite people you don't know in to your home. It is unsafe for you and your family.

Face the Facts

You will not get along with everyone you meet. Take your time when choosing the people you are going to work with—both internally and externally. You wouldn't marry someone just on a recommendation, and most marriages that begin a day after the couple meets don't last long. Make sure you like your team members enough to spend a lot of time with them.

Background Checks

After you have interviewed your prospective employee, he has answered all your questions to your satisfaction, and you think he might fit into your business, now is the time to run a background check. There are several companies you can contact, and the cost will run you $20 to $150, depending on what kind of check you want. Why should you run background checks? Even though a person's past employer may have had no problems with him and the guy may seem on the up and up, you need to know if he is paying his child support or if he has been arrested for substance abuse or selling illicit drugs in the community. You need to know if a person can be trusted or if he needs to be watched a little more closely than other employees.

Also consider looking up your prospective employee on the Internet. You might be amazed at the information you can find on another person. I did an Internet search on one of our former employees and discovered there was a warrant out for his arrest.

Training

Once you have hired your employees, you will want to give them some sort of training if needed, at the very minimum an orientation. If you have hired more than one or two employees, you might want to have a group orientation where you will give them your company manual and talk about what is included in it. When you give your employee your manual, have him sign and date a roster sheet stating that he received it. If he should come back later and say he didn't receive one, you can show him his signature and remind him that he did. Tell your employees to read through the manual later even though you are discussing parts of it. You might forget to tell them something, and if they read it, they will cover all the bases.

For those who are new to painting, the training will be on the job. You may start by having a new employee help you set up, move ladders, and after showing him how to tape, tape off window and door casings. There is always sanding and puttying to be done, and this is another good job for a beginner. After he gets into the groove of that, add one more responsibility to his tasks. Teach him how to roll walls after they've been cut in and then teach him how to cut in.

Probationary Period

It's a good idea to set a probationary period of six weeks to six months. Tell your employee up front about the probationary period if you are looking for someone to work for you full time. Six weeks to six months should give you enough time to evaluate your new employee's work habits, see if there are any problems between him and other employees, and determine if he is going to be a valuable asset to your business. If problems arise, give the employee a warning and remind him of his probationary period in writing. If the situation doesn't improve, let that employee go and find another.

Benefits

While you are required to withhold taxes and carry workers' comp on your employees, as a small business you may not be able to provide all the benefits you would like to for your employees. Health care may be all you can afford, and if that's it, then that's it. Don't knock yourself out by trying to compete against a larger painting company across town. Give your employees what you can, and don't sweat the rest.

Pay Raises

As your business grows and you pick up more work, you may be able to and want to pay your employees more. For instance, if you hired an employee at minimum wage, he has passed the probationary period, and you see him as an asset to your business, you may want to increase his hourly wage by a dollar. You don't have to announce it to the rest of your crew unless you are giving them a pay raise as well. A good rule of thumb is to let your employees know that hard work is rewarded, but at your discretion.

Letting Employees Go

This is one of the more unpleasant aspects of owning and running your own business, but there are instances when you will have to let employees go. In today's society, not only is the firing unpleasant, but it can also be a fearful time. You never know if you might be sued or in some rare cases even killed. There are, however, legitimate reasons for letting someone go—habitual tardiness, continued absenteeism, dishonesty, a lack of cooperation with you and the rules, or an inability to do the work.

Before you fire someone, though, be sure that you know what your employee's rights are, that you have given adequate written warning for infractions, and that the firing is for something the employee knew was against company policy. You don't want to set yourself up for a lawsuit.

Fire the person in some private location, not in front of other workers. They will hear about it soon enough. Give the person his last paycheck and be civil no matter how difficult it may be for you. Always tell the person specifically why he is being fired. He will probably already know, but by your telling him, he will have no cause to wonder. Tell him you are sorry things didn't work out, shake his hand, and wish him luck for the future.

There will also be times when you have to let people go, not because you want to, but because the workload is not big enough to have extra employees. If this occurs, alert your workers early enough so they can find other jobs. Most will know because when you hired them you told them their work was temporary because of the work season. Talk to these people individually or in a group. For those who are your summer workers, tell them you appreciate them and you hope they will work for you again next year, if you liked their work. You might want to give them a time to contact you when you will be hiring again. By doing this you will already be making contacts to build your next seasonal workforce.

07

Ethical, Legal, and Safety Issues

In the house painting business, there are certain ethical, legal, and safety issues that must be addressed. Most people go into this business thinking that all they have to do is slap some paint on a wall and their job is over. That is far from the case. In this chapter we are going to discuss issues a house painter may face over the years, how to avert disaster before it strikes, how to deal with it if it does, and how to move on.

Ethical Issues

The word *ethics* comes from the Greek word *ethos* and according to the dictionary means "a system of moral principles governing the appropriate conduct for a person or group." For businesses that translates to a code of conduct or a set of guidelines in which they operate. An unethical business can only operate for so long. Sooner or later unethical practices will catch up with the owner. Stories abound of painters who have lost their credibility and their livelihood because of their unscrupulous business practices. Nobody wants to be the "ethics" police, but the lack of ethics in businesses today has caused a serious crisis in the world economy. You may say, "I'm a small business." That is true, but if you work on ethical issues in your business, it may transcend into other businesses. At the very least, you may instill in your employees ethical practices that will follow them wherever they go. One person can make a difference. Discussing some of the problems that happened in the past may give you pause to think about these issues as you build your business in the future.

In Dealing with Clients

Since clients or customers will be your source of income, you need to treat them fairly and be up front with them about the services and work you will be

> **From the Trenches**
>
> One new trend among house painting companies is to offer a "limited warranty" to customers on their paint jobs. These can range from a three-month touch-up job to a thirty-day change of color. Be very careful when offering a warranty and be very specific about the type of warranty work you will do. Offer what you feel comfortable with and no more.
>
> To learn more about this trend, visit www.house-painting-info.com and search for "warranty."

providing. Set one price for your services and perform quality work whether you are painting a $2 million home or a $50,000 home. Hold to your warranty, if you give one, and follow up with your customers as you promised you would.

Do not share your clients' personal information with others, like selling their names and addresses to marketing firms or phone banks for advertising calls. That information is for you to use. By sending a letter or postcard to your clients once a year, you will keep your name in front of them and they won't feel as though they are being harassed.

In Dealing with Employees

When you have employees, there are several things you need to provide—fair promotional opportunities, a safe work environment, and payment of their salaries in a timely manner.

Fair promotional opportunities mean giving your employees the ability to get ahead. That can translate into taking on more responsibility at a single job site or perhaps running a job on his own. Of course, with promotion comes an increase in salary and maybe extra benefits. Judge each employee on his own merit and promote him accordingly. Don't discriminate between men and women or young and old.

Providing a safe work environment not only includes physical safety, but mental safety as well. This means nipping sexual harassment in the bud before it starts. Watch for cliques forming, and if there are workplace bullies, put them in their place before the situation gets out of hand.

As the boss it is your responsibility to be respectful of your employees. If you can't be respectful of the person you hire, don't hire him. Your employees will take their cues from you.

Finally for this section, pay your employees when you say you will, be it weekly, biweekly, or monthly. Nothing is more disheartening, discouraging, or troubling than working but not getting paid. Your employees have bills to pay just the same as you. You promised them a certain amount of money at a specific time for a span of work. Keep your promises. David pays his employees before he pays us. A paycheck keeps employees loyal and keeps them doing their work.

In Dealing with Your Creditors

You will owe money to people when you buy paint, supplies, vehicles, or equipment. Pay your creditors in a timely manner. Strive not to be late. If an unforeseeable situation happens and you are going to be late on a payment, call the creditor and explain. There may be instances when you don't get paid or your client is late paying you. Tell your creditors. If you are honest with them, they will typically work with you until you can pay. Remember to call. Don't leave them hanging and not knowing what's going on.

In Dealing with Your Business Associates

If you have partners or when reporting to a member of your internal team, be honest with the assessment of your business. When work is slow, let them know. Also let them know what you are doing to pick up more business. Are you doing some extra marketing? Are you bidding jobs? Are you looking to expand your skills?

On the flip side, don't cook the books to make it look as if your business is doing better than it is. Let your business speak for itself in terms of the bottom line. If you cheat on paper, it will eventually catch up with you.

In Dealing with Your Family

Sometimes you will have so much work it will seem you hardly see your spouse, if you are married, and children, if you have any. Remind them that you are building a business and there will come a time when you can't make it to every Little League game and piano recital. Try to attend, but if you can't, explain why you couldn't make it. Don't act as though an event doesn't exist in your family's life because work kept you from making it.

At other times work will be slow and money will be tight, especially if you haven't planned for the slow times. If you see work will be getting slow, warn your family in advance. In some cases this may be to your advantage. If you have been working so much and haven't had a lot of time to spend with your family, you might want to use this time to catch up. Plan to take a vacation or visit extended family members during your downtime. If you spend time with your family while you are off, they will appreciate the time you work.

In Dealing with the Government

While you may wince when you read this and wonder what it has to do with business ethics, dealing with the government is a big part of business ethics. There are certain rules and regulations—local, state, and federal—that must be followed when you own and operate your business. Licenses and permits must be purchased in some cases. When these are required, bite the bullet and buy them. Pay your taxes when you are required to. This will protect you from penalties in the long run and give credibility to your business. How do you feel when you hear of a business that has blown off getting the proper paperwork and neglected paying its taxes?

In Dealing with Competitors

Don't use underhanded or unscrupulous practices when dealing with other house painting businesses. Show them the respect you would like shown to you. Of course they are your competition and you are trying to get work just as they are, but that's all another business is. Don't talk to clients about a specific competitor's grade of work, any rumors you may have heard about your competitors or what they charge. Your clients are adults. They can ask questions and make up their minds about your competition themselves. Besides you may wind up sounding like a fool.

You might even want to approach your competitors and get to know them. There may be instances when you could help one another out. You can throw them some work if you become overwhelmed, and they can throw you some if they have more than they can handle. By getting to know your competitors on a personal level, you might find out they are hardworking people just like you.

In Dealing with the Environment

During your years in the business, you will be faced with environmental issues when disposing of certain paints and other liquids. The best rule of thumb is to follow the government (local or federal) standards for cleanup and disposal. For instance, if you have a spill, there are certain ways the government wants you to clean up. With empty or partially filled paint receptacles, you can't just throw them out with the family trash. Anything that is liquid, you must dispose of at a hazardous waste disposal site. Check the Environmental Protection Agency's website at www.epa.gov/osw to find out how and where to dispose of your materials.

You can dispose of your paint in other ways, too. When you finish with a job, leave the remaining paint at the house for touch-ups. If you calculated your bid correctly, you should only have a little paint left. You could also leave the lids off the paint cans, let your paint dry out, and then throw it away. Or you could pour the remaining paint out on a piece of Visqueen plastic sheeting, let your paint dry, and then roll it up and throw it away.

Don't store your paint and cleaning supplies near a heat source. They could start a fire and release harmful chemicals into the air or, heaven forbid, cause an explosion. Even with the new paint standards, there are still certain risks. Check out the Environmental Protection Agency's website to learn more.

Finally, when cleaning your tools and equipment, make sure that the water run-off is not going to get into freshwater or drinking water supplies. Besides destroying the environment for the rest of us, you can rack up hefty fines if you are caught.

Legal Issues

When starting and running a business, you are going to face certain legal issues. These issues will need to be addressed and in most cases, the sooner, the better for you and your business. If you don't take care of these issues, court costs can not only run you a lot of money but they can also destroy your business. While some of the topics covered here may not be relevant to your company, you need to consider these issues when operating a business.

Business Type

If you have not decided which business type your company will operate under, you need to decide now. While you may be working on the assumption that your business is a sole proprietorship, it is always best to investigate the four business types and know what advantages and disadvantages each one offers. Basic information can be found in chapter 2. Talk to an accountant to get more information and to make sure you are filing your business taxes according to the business type you have chosen. If you have filed in the wrong category, you could be paying too many taxes or not enough.

Paying and Filing Taxes and Reports

When you own a small business, you are required to not only turn in year-end reports to the Internal Revenue Service, but quarterly reports as well. If you have employees, you have to report how much they make, take out federal and state withholding and FICA (Medicare and Social Security) taxes for each employee from his paycheck and then report it. If you fail to report and pay your quarterly taxes, you can face a huge fine. If you fail to report the correct amount of income your business made, you can also face a fine. When dealing with the IRS, it is better to be safe than sorry. Follow the rules. Turn your reports in when they are required.

Working with Immigrants

In construction you will find plenty of immigrants willing to work on job sites. What you have to look out for are those who are in the country illegally. The U.S. Immigration and Customs Enforcement, also known as ICE, has been cracking down on small business that employ illegal immigrants, and those employers found in violation of immigration regulations can be fined or have civil or in some cases criminal charges filed against them. ICE does what is called an immigration audit periodically on businesses, and if you are found to be in violation, whether you are aware of your employees' status or not, the agency can shut your business down.

If you decide to hire an immigrant, make sure that you have your I-9 forms up to date. After hiring an employee, employers are required to get I-9 forms completed within three days. You must also get the employee's basic information, like name, address, Social Security number, and date of birth, as well as a form stating that the person has the government's permission to be working in this country. You then take this information and verify your employee's eligibility to work with the government. You can use the E-verify system on the U.S. Citizenship and Immigration Service's website at www.uscis.gov. Make sure you verify the employee's status, as once again if you don't, you can face stiff penalties and maybe even jail time. If you cannot verify your employee's status, you have to let him go to avoid liability yourself. An immigration attorney can help you move through the ins and outs of hiring immigrants. Be sure to follow his recommendations.

Employee Lawsuits

You always have to be aware that there is a chance an employee will sue you. Two of the biggest claims are discrimination and wrongful termination. To combat these claims an employer must be proactive, which means making sure that all of your employees have guidelines in their hands as to what discrimination is and that you as an employer must enforce the rules and regulations regarding discrimination. When firing someone, you must make sure that the termination is legitimately related to work and not personal. When you give warnings alerting the employee that his job is in danger, it is always a good idea to do so in writing and to keep a copy yourself. You must establish a precedent for the actions you are taking.

Other reasons for employee lawsuits include wage theft, workplace injury, false accusations, and being overlooked for promotion. Always be on your guard and make sure that you have resolutions to problems before they grow.

Lawsuits from Clients

When doing exteriors, you will inevitably work with an airless sprayer. To avoid costly lawsuits, avoid spraying on windy days. You can get overspray on houses and vehicles in the immediate area. In some cases, the overspray paint can be buffed off, but there are occasions when a person whose property has been damaged wants a new paint job or even a brand new car. So watch where and when you spray.

Safety Issues

On any job site there is always a chance of injury. On a construction job site, the odds go even higher that someone may get hurt or even die. The Occupational Safety and Health Administration has set guidelines to try to minimize injuries and deaths, yet accidents continue to happen. Before going out or starting any job, you need to visit OSHA's website (www.osha.gov) and read up on all the rules and regulations.

Besides you or your employee getting injured, others may get injured as well, since house painters work in homes, sometimes new and sometimes occupied. The following are some areas that house painters have to be particularly mindful of as they work on houses:

Minimizing Falls

Falls from any height can lead to injuries like sprained ankles, broken bones, twisted backs, and in some cases, death. By being aware of your environment and taking a few precautions, serious injuries can be avoided.

Let's look at ladders first. When setting up your ladders inside, use the A-frame version. Make sure your ladder is all the way out and locked into position. If you are the only one working on a job, do not reach out away from your ladder. Even though it may be sitting on solid ground, the ladder could tip and fall. If someone is working with you, have him hold the ladder in place. While you may think it would be easier to reach a corner by stretching than to get down and move the ladder, moving the ladder would be better than falling and breaking your wrist, putting you out of work for three or more months.

When working on the exterior of a house, you will more than likely use extension ladders. You can use the A-frames, but sometimes they are more cumbersome than extensions. Besides, A-frames only go so high, and on exteriors, you will often need ten to twelve feet of ladder. These ladders lean up against the side of a house and allow you to reach underneath the eaves of the roof. Make sure that when you set these ladders, they are planted on level ground. This is especially important if you are working alone. If the ground is not level, try to make it level, by putting a flat board underneath a leg or building up the dirt around the leg. If you have to build up an area, get someone to work with you and hold the ladder while you climb. One slight shift of your makeshift brace could send you tumbling. You should make it a policy to have someone available to hold ladders if you or your employees have to climb higher than six feet in any case.

You may never have to use scaffolding on a job site, but if you do, make sure you know how to set it up and all the components are locked in place. Once again, do not lean over railings, and make sure you are secure and tied off if working higher than six feet.

When working on a job, make sure your tools are kept picked up and left in one area. Not only does this let you know where your tools are, but people then won't trip over them.

There always will be the occasional spill. Clean it up immediately even if it has fallen on your drop cloth. If you or an employee steps in it and then walks on an uncovered floor, you will track the paint and also risk slipping. Paint is slippery until it is dry. By cleaning up the mess right away, you can eliminate accidents in the future.

If someone should fall, it is best to keep the person lying still and dial 911. Stories abound of people getting up, saying they are all right, and then dying from internal bleeding within a few hours or suffering from serious neck or spine injuries within a week or two. It's always better to be safe than sorry.

Avoid Electrocution

Typically, by the time the painters arrive on a job site, the electricity is on whether the house is new or existing. This is definitely no time to let your guard down. Painters tell stories of getting "bit" by wires hanging down from ceilings or out of walls, and then there are the stories of painters who have died because some of their equipment hit "hot lines." The best way to avoid electrocution is to use safe equipment and stay away from power sources.

With equipment, buy fiberglass ladders and paint poles. Fiberglass doesn't conduct a charge the way metal does. If you should slip and fall into a live wire outside or inside, your chances of survival are much greater. When faced with dangling wires that you must lift or move, use either a piece of wood or plastic. Also, make sure your feet are dry when dealing with electricity. If it has been raining or you have been washing equipment and your feet are wet, wait until they dry before moving wires or dealing with electrical sockets.

If the worst should happen and someone is electrocuted on the job, do not run up, grab him, and try to pull him off the wires. When someone is electrocuted, the current pulls that person into the source. If you grab a person being electrocuted, you can be drawn in and electrocuted as well. The best thing to do is cut the power, and if that isn't an option, grab a piece of wood or your fiberglass paint pole and knock the person away from the current source.

Head Injuries

Most head injuries can be avoided by simply wearing a hard hat. OSHA requires hard hats on some jobs, but as a house painter you may not always need to wear one. In the instances when you are working on a new construction where beams are exposed and the electricians or plumbers are still working on a floor above you, it would be wise to bite the bullet and wear a hard hat. Workers never know when a beam will slip and fall, and then there is the occasional hammer or wrench that can fall from a flight of stairs or off a beam.

Cuts and Bruises

If you don't have a first-aid kit, get one. When you are on the job, you never know when someone will slice a finger, get splinters, or suffer a host of other injuries. By having a first-aid kit you will have access to band-aids, topical antibiotic, and other bandaging supplies. If someone does get cut on the job or steps on a nail, make sure the person has had a tetanus shot within the last ten years or gets one immediately.

Always make sure you have access to a phone system where you can dial 911. If you are working in an area without 911 coverage, make sure you have a list of emergency numbers available so you can call and get help right away.

Fume Illness

Even though paint manufacturers have been working on making paints safer, there is no way of getting around fumes. In your business you will run across individuals who have no problems with the fumes, but people who suffer from asthma or some sort of allergy, pregnant women, or sick children will all need to be warned about the fresh smell of paint as they will probably have problems with the fumes.

It is a good idea to inform your clients about the fumes at the beginning of the job. You don't want to make anyone sick and have to rush him to the hospital, or have a pregnant woman miscarry or deliver early. These medical problems have been known to happen after painters work, so check to make sure there are no health issues you need to be aware of.

There are a few steps you can take to minimize the danger fumes may cause. First, if you can, open windows to air out the house as you paint. In the winter that might not be an option, but for the other three seasons, this shouldn't be a problem. This will also help you and your employees as you move through a certain job. The second option is to use fans. Fans help move the air around, thus dissipating the

Tips That Make Cents

If you need industrial or commercial fans to air out a location or to help dry paint and you don't have the money to purchase them right away, check out renting them. Your local hardware or home improvement store has them to rent sometimes for as low as $10 a day.

fumes. The ideal situation would be to have the windows open and the fans running at the same time. This moves fumes out quickly.

Freedom Painting has several industrial floor fans. They are made of solid metal construction and can run in forward mode to blow air or reverse mode to suck air out. Industrial fans come in floor models or pedestal models. These fans can cost $80 to $400 depending on what model you buy. Northern Safety has many fans you can choose from online, or check with your local home supply store.

08 Marketing Your Business

So now that you have decided house painting is what you want to pursue, you've bought some equipment, and have your internal and external team in place, let's look at ways you can market your business to pick up clients. You may think that all you have to do is place a few ads in the newspaper. While that might work to get a few jobs, there are other activities you need to continually do to build your business and make it a success. Marketing is more than just ads. Marketing encompasses everything you do to get clients. Advertising is only one of the tools you use to get those marketing results.

If the wheels are turning in your head and you are thinking that you want to paint and not be a salesman, you need to consider your thoughts on marketing before reading any further. Do you dread having to talk to people to get work? Do you hate salesmen and have you promised yourself never to be one? Are you not sure what you want to tell people about your services? If you answered yes to any of these questions, then you need to *change* how you look at marketing.

First, think of the services you are offering people as an opportunity for them and not an obligation. After all, you are offering to change the look of their home, to freshen it up, to give it a new vibe. Instead of thinking about "getting work," think about what you can do for people, how you can make the environment they live in better.

Second, consider that when you are speaking to someone, you are offering information, communicating instead of manipulating. This makes a big difference. By communicating how you can help improve someone's living space, you will grow more confident in offering your services.

Third, think about contact, not just activity or busy work. As you will see, many ways exist to get the word out about your business. But which ways are the best at reaching potential customers? How is the word about your business reaching customers? Is there a buzz about you in the community or are there just ads? What are you doing differently that causes people to sit up and take notice?

Compared with other businesses, you as a house painter are at a disadvantage. You don't have a physical storefront where people can come in, pick an item off the shelf, pay for it, and leave. You are in a service business; therefore, you have to reach out to people and tell them what you can do for them and their homes.

You've got to tell people about your services. If you don't tell them you do specialty walls, how are they going to know? If you paint concrete floors, stain and lacquer wood, or texture walls, you have to let potential clients know.

To get the word out about your business, you have to decide on your marketing plan. Yes, you must have a plan. And in that plan you need to ask yourself how do you want to market your business. How much are you willing and able to spend on marketing right away? At first, all you may be able to do is get your business cards and the domain name for your website. That's all right, just plan to take steps next month and then the next month and then the month after that. If your plan is to do two things a month, by the end of the year, you will have made a lot of contacts and gotten a lot of word out about your business. Action creates a snowball effect.

Before you make any decisions, though, let's take a look at all the aspects you need to consider before settling on a strategy.

Who Is Your Competition?

While you may think the answer to this question is simple—another painter—that's not entirely the correct answer. Another painter may turn in a bid for the job, but if you have a good reputation and provide a quality job at competitive rates, there really won't be any competition from another painter. With that said, you have greater hurdles than another painter competing against you for work.

The Economy

When the economy takes a downturn, everyone starts cutting back and with good reason. If you had to choose between painting your living room and making your house payment, which would you choose? If you live in an area where a plant or a big business has closed, the last thing on people's minds is getting their house painted. In cases like this, it wouldn't matter how little you charged to paint houses; if people don't have money, they won't want a paint job.

Customer's Time

On the flip side, sometimes potential clients are so busy they don't have time to make arrangements with you to have their house painted. If they travel a lot, it honestly may not work out for them to hire a painter, especially if they have to make arrangements to meet you to let you in or need to move furniture around. That's one reason you have to build a reputation for being prompt, having integrity, and getting the work done.

Other Painter's Reputations

It is an awful truth that in the past painters, especially house painters, have not had stellar reputations. It is not the majority, but as in all things, one bad potato can ruin a whole bag. There have been painters who have only half completed jobs, stolen from clients while on the job, and cased houses and come back after jobs were completed to rob the homeowners. If people in your area have been burned by a painter, you will be fighting a tough battle getting people to trust you to come into their homes.

Self-Home Improvement Craze

Today, more and more people are making improvements to their homes by themselves. They go to the home improvement store, buy some paint, and make painting their home a weekend project. Some people were raised to do projects themselves, and that's what they do. Other people enjoy taking the time to paint their homes the colors they want, when they want. People also try to save money, and when they can paint their house for $200 instead of paying you $1,000, they are going to choose the cheaper route.

Customer's Other Priorities

Perhaps your potential customers have built a new addition to their home and decided to paint it themselves because they have to use the money they might spend on a painter on plumbing, electrical work, carpeting, or furniture. This happens more often than you think.

The way to beat your competition is to know about these issues and deal with them accordingly. Dealing may mean you look in another section of town for work or learn to specialize in an area where people *need* your services and can't do what you do themselves. Think about this competition and figure out ways to overcome a potential client's objections. This will go a long way in getting you customers.

What Are People Looking for from Their House Painting Job?

As you start talking to people about paint jobs, you will find seven points coming up in your conversations again and again. Most people have certain expectations when upgrading, beautifying, or changing the interior or exterior of their homes. Following are the seven issues we have heard discussed the most:

1. **Quality Job:** You may think this is a given, but believe it or not, there are not only awful paint jobs out there but terrible ones, too. The next time you are in a home, look at the details of the paint job. Is there paint on the window casings? Are the colors on the walls even or can you see drips or roller marks? Does the wall paint join the ceiling paint seamlessly? You'll be amazed at what you see when you start looking. Clients see it, too. A professional job looks totally different from an amateur one.

2. **A Change:** While most clients will want to stick with the white standard for their interior house color, some clients are ready to change their wall color

Around the Paint Bucket

Just as there are doctors who specialize in one area of medicine, like heart medicine, cancer, or delivering babies, there are painters who specialize in certain areas, like wood work or specialty walls. These specialty doctors make more money on average than general or family practitioners. So do the specialty painters.

drastically. They may want their nursery painted pink or blue or their bathroom or bedroom purple. You will also have clients who want to have wallpaper removed to have a flat wall painted or those with flat walls who want a textured focus wall. Be prepared for all requests.

3. **Reasonable Price:** Most people know they get what they pay for, and while they may be looking for a bargain, if your reputation precedes you, your customers will be happy to pay your price as long as you haven't priced them out of the market. You can charge more for specialty walls or for a lot of prep work, like removing wallpaper. But mostly people will have a budget, and they will want to stay within the confines of that budget. So don't overprice and don't underprice. Keep your prices in the mid-range so people of all budgets can afford you.

4. **Job Done in a Timely Manner:** Let's face it, clients don't want you in their homes or around their homes for weeks on end. Your job is to get in and get your job done as soon as possible. Your clients' homes are torn up while you're working. They want to return to normal as soon as possible.

5. **Integrity:** This is simple and should be in your code of ethics. Say what you are going to do and then do it. If you give a quote, then stick to that price. If you have done your homework, you will know that the price of a certain kind

Getting the Job Done

We were shocked over the past summer to watch a crew of six take a month to paint a single-story double condo unit. My husband and one of his employees painted a two-story double condo unit with two back balconies and two front bridges in three days. Even more shocking was that, after this crew of six packed up and left, they hadn't gotten the eaves of the house or the fireplace edging on the roof painted. We are still wondering what they did for a full thirty days.

Quality service includes not only getting the job done right the first time, but following up after the job is done. It involves calling your customer, arriving on time, and working. You shouldn't be talking on your phone all morning, taking extended breaks, or leaving jobs unfinished. Give your client what he is paying for—you doing a job.

of paint is going higher and you can figure that into your estimate. If you haven't prepared for that possibility and the paint goes up, you should eat the added price. That's only fair to your client.

6. **Safety:** With allergies and other respiratory problems prevalent in homes, some clients will want to know what is in the paint you are spreading on their walls. While most paints today are nontoxic, some still cause allergic reactions. Know which ones can cause harm so you can warn your clients. In some cases, you might have to recommend that they leave their house for a while until the fumes dissipate. You will of course be responsible for airing the house out, but when you lock the door, there will still be fumes that linger.

    Also, always be on the alert for lead problems, as your clients will be. Today, lead has been removed from paint, but in older houses you may still find it prevalent on the walls, door casings, and window casings.

7. **Environmental Responsibility:** As more and more people become environmentally aware, you may be asked about the products you use. Who makes them? What are they made of? Has the manufacturing company tested the products on animals? Is the manufacturing company environmentally responsible? How and where do you dispose of your leftover products? Be prepared to answer these questions and perhaps more. If you show you are concerned about the environment, people's safety, and doing a good job for people, word will spread about you and your business. This will be the key to your success.

Now, let's get down to the nitty-gritty of marketing.

Marketing . . . Where to Start

Before you do anything else, get business cards made, if you haven't already. Besides you standing in front of someone, these little cards can be your best selling tool. When you talk to people, selling your service, they may not need you right away. If you hit it off, they may want to call you in the future for a paint job, so the first thing they do is ask for a business card. If you don't have one available, how will these people know how to get in touch with you when they are ready for a job to be done?

Business cards don't have to be complex or expensive. You can put a small logo on something like a paint brush, your name, and your contact information like address, phone number, website, and e-mail address. In your neighborhood, you can probably find a place to design and print your cards for under $50. But don't forget to check online. Vistaprint runs specials all the time. You can get 250 business cards for free, and if you want to buy more, the fees are nominal. It currently sells five hundred cards for $10. Vistaprint has templates and some clip art, and is easy to work with to prepare the business card you would like. Check out its website at www.vistaprint .com to see the latest offers.

Networking

Networking is the process of meeting people face to face and building a relationship with the hopes of getting business to develop your company. This word-of-mouth marketing technique is powerful and will no doubt be your main way of getting business. Why? When people meet you and you build a relationship with them, chances are they will like you. If they like you and know what you do, they are more likely to call on your services and recommend you and your services to people they know.

Networking is important as you try to build your business. Through networking, you can tell people about your business without feeling as if you are being a salesman because in a networking situation people will ask what you do. You tell them, pass out your card, get theirs, and move on. It may cost you a couple of hundred dollars to join an organization and some of your time, but once you are known in the community, you will start picking up leads.

While networking is a popular way to build your business and you will be able to pick up clients by doing it, there are some downsides. Networking has to be worked at week after week, month after month. It isn't a one-time event. To build those business relationships, you have to see people over and over again and talk to them over and over again. If your work schedule is full, you may find it difficult to attend meetings and thus reduce the effectiveness of this particular marketing strategy. Building your business through networking takes time. You may get a client right away, or you may not get one for six months to a year, so if you need clients in a hurry, this may not be the best way to go.

If you decide to network, which you probably will in one form or another sooner or later, don't lose heart if nothing seems to be happening at first. If you believe in what you are doing and are working to build relationships with people who need and can afford your painting services, you will be fine. A lot of the success of networking happens in the background. The more people see you, the more familiar you become to them. The more familiar people become with you, the more they feel they can trust you.

Following are a few tips to keep in mind as you begin networking:

- *Network in a productive fish pond.* When you start networking, go to meetings where you can meet a lot of people who might be interested in your services or people who know people who might be interested in your services—perhaps there is a builders association in your area where home building contractors go to network or a small business association where small business owners get together and talk about business issues. Attend these meetings a few times and decide if they will be beneficial for you. If so, keep attending. If not, look around for another group to network with. You can network around the clock, but if you are not in a place where you can get clients, it won't benefit you.
- *Attend meetings regularly.* Being listed in an organization's directory or attending the annual Christmas party probably won't get you many clients. Out of sight is out of mind. If you don't attend meetings but once a year, how is someone going to remember your name or business? You have to get involved, or show up at the very least.
- *Become involved in the group or organization.* Another way to get people to start recognizing you is to get involved. Serve on a committee or become

Cost Versus Reward

Think belonging to an organization or attending meetings is a frivolous waste of time and money? If you are in the right place at the right time, you can cultivate leads that can turn into business. Worried about the cost of belonging to one of these groups? Don't be. The cost of admission will be well worth it, especially if you pick up work. If you get one job, you will have made your yearly dues back. Besides, if you keep accurate records, any fees or dues can be counted as business expenses and are tax deductible.

one of the organization's officers. You don't have to serve as president, but by doing something in the organization, you will get your name known.

■ *Always arrive early and leave late.* Most networking takes place before a meeting or afterward. Some people will come early because they have to leave right after the meeting, and some will stay after the meeting for a while because they arrived late. If you stay before and after the meeting, you can meet and talk to both groups of people. Let's face it, not much networking goes on during the meeting as the speaker is talking or the business of the group is being discussed. With that said, don't arrive too early or stay too long after the meeting. Ten to fifteen minutes is usually ideal. This gives you enough time to say hello to people you have met before, meet new people, and finish up conversations you might have started earlier.

■ *Make it a point to meet new people.* As new people come into the group, be sure to introduce yourself, find out what they do, give them a business card, and get one of theirs. You never know when they will be beneficial to you and bring you new business. Not only does this expand your business outreach, but it lets you get acquainted with all the incoming members of the group. If a new person is somewhat shy, he or she may feel welcomed to the group simply by your act of going up to them. Making someone feel comfortable can lead to business.

■ *Focus on one person at a time.* Ever been to a meeting and the person talking to you keeps looking around or over your shoulder for someone else? That's a sign that the person isn't really interested in what you are saying.

So, when you talk to someone, give him or her your full attention, look him in the eye, and listen to what he is saying. After the conversation, you can look for someone else to talk to or focus on what is going on across the room.

I realize situations may arise when you really need to speak with someone else or the person you are talking to is going on about nothing. In that case, excuse yourself politely by saying, "I look forward to seeing you at future meetings," or "Let's talk more later," or "I see someone else I need to speak with. If you'd excuse me," or "It's been a pleasure meeting you."

On the flip side, don't buzz from one person to another. You can offer quick hellos or slaps on the back to regulars and then seek out others you want to talk to. You may not have the time to meet and greet everyone. A good rule of thumb is to meet one new person and then have an advanced conversation with another person each meeting. This allows you to meet new people but also get to know some of the other members of the group. Sometimes groups are so large, there is no way you can meet or share meaningful conversations with everyone, so pace yourself. In the long run, you will do better by talking sincerely to one person than by carrying on hit-and-run conversations with the whole room.

- *Make sure you carry plenty of business cards.* Take an ample supply of business cards, pass them out, and collect cards from people you meet. These will grow into your contact list, contacts you can get leads from to build your business.

  Collect business cards from appropriate contacts. Write down notes about where you met the person and anything you might have learned about him or his business. You can use that information later when you contact him. If you learn someone has a sick child, ask how that child is doing, by name, the next time you talk to that person. People are impressed when you remember the names of their family members and ask about their well-being. It shows them you care.

- *Wear your name tag proudly.* Put your first and last name on your name tag and the name of your business. Wear it on the right side, so when people shake your hand they can see it easily.

- *Jump in to the foray yourself.* There is an old saying, "You can lead a horse to water, but you can't make him drink." The same is true for networking.

You can get a businessman to a meeting, but you can't make him introduce himself. Let's say you've been invited to a networking meeting, but instead of mingling, you sit at a table and wait for people to come to you. Maybe you are expecting the person who invited you to take you around and introduce you? What if that person is late to the meeting or doesn't come at all? Are you going to let this opportunity pass you by? I hope not.

You may be saying, I'm not an outgoing person, or I don't like meeting new people. While you may be shy, your body language and your lack of social ability may be saying to others, "I'm better than you are" or "You are unimportant to me." So get off your duff and start introducing yourself. More likely than not, when you stick out your hand, smile, and say hello, the person you are directing your attention to will respond. You can start your conversation with "I don't think we've met." You don't have to be king of the court or belle of the ball. All you have to be is friendly. Beyond that, one of the best ways to get people to talk to you is to get them to talk about themselves. Some simple conversation questions might be: "What do you do?" "How long have you been coming to these meetings?" "What drew you to this group?" "Do you know tonight's speaker?" or "Tell me about your business."

Where to Find Networking Opportunities

Word of mouth will always be your best marketing tool, but where do you find people to talk to about your business. Here are a few suggestions.

Friends and Relatives

When you talk to friends and relatives about your business, you are networking. These people will probably be the easiest for you to talk to because you know them already. Don't talk incessantly about your business; that can be a bore, but let them know about your new venture. They can pass the word along to people they know, and in turn those people may pass along your name to the people they know.

Informal Networking

You can and should let people know what you do at your church, social gatherings, and sporting events. Always carry your business cards, so you can pass them out. Don't be overbearing; in a casual way, just let people know what you do.

Another way to network within these groups is to sponsor a sports team or offer to bring cups or napkins to social events—and of course have your business name and logo printed on them. This can become expensive so check out prices before you volunteer.

Home and Garden Shows

Participate in home and garden shows. You can meet a lot of people at these events, and typically the people who come to these events are thinking about fixing up their homes. Besides meeting and talking to people, you should have flyers at your booth and as an added bonus, a giveaway like rulers or pens with your business name, phone number, and website printed on them. People will approach your booth if for no other reason than to pick up a freebie.

Getting into these shows can be expensive and may take a while. They tend to fill up fast. Sometimes they are booked two or three years in advance. When that happens, they will put you on a list and contact you if a spot opens up. We once waited five years to get into a show. Prices can run from $500 to $2,000 for a three-day event depending on how big the show is, so be prepared. Those prices are just for the event. They don't include what you will need to get yourself—a banner, flyers, and giveaways if you decide to use them.

At these events you can pass out flyers, meet and greet, and get to know the people of your community. Remember, a lot of people too are looking for bargains at these events, so be sure to send attendees home with some sort of incentive to call you like a 30 percent off coupon good for thirty days after the home and garden show ends.

Organizations

Organizations are a great way to meet people and get the buzz started about your business. Contact neighborhood associations. Call their local president and arrange to meet him or her. Tell him what you do and leave some business cards. If you make a good impression, you might be asked to speak at the next neighborhood meeting.

Join professional organizations and associations in your area like the chamber of commerce, home-based business association, local subcontractors association, or a small business association. Women can join the National Association of Women Business Owners. Real estate agents tend to hang out at chamber meetings, and you can meet building contractors at subcontractors' get-togethers.

Community Groups and Clubs

Check out community clubs like the Kiwanis, Rotary, Lions, and Leads Clubs. People join these organizations to become a part of the community and network.

Free Consultations

Probably the best way to meet people and get a conversation started about what you do is to offer free consultations or free estimates. When you get a call from someone, go meet with them, hear what they want painted, and then give them a written price.

Some More Networking Tips

Don't let opportunities pass you by. If you are talking to someone who sounds interested in you doing work for him, set up a time right then for the two of you to get together so you can give him an estimate. If someone gives you a referral, contact the person that day to set up an appointment. Don't wait. If you do, you may lose a client. At the very least, if you can't meet with the person the next day, set up a time to meet the following week and then be there.

Stay in touch with your clients or prospective clients. After you have given someone your estimate, wait a few days; if you don't hear back, give the person a call. Be polite, ask if he has had time to think about the estimate and if he was ready to get the job started. Don't be forceful or indignant if the person you gave the estimate to can't do the job now.

Networking is about building relationships. The best way to do that is to treat everyone you meet with respect, show them you are interested in their needs, and be considerate of their time when dealing with them.

Send thank you notes for referrals. This may sound old-fashioned, but there is nothing more personal than a handwritten thank you note. It makes the receiver feel important and lets him know how much you appreciate his helping you out with your business.

> "You have to be talked about to get work."—*Georgia O'Keeffe*

Other Forms of Marketing That May Prove Helpful

While you may think you have exhausted all of your marketing options, there are other activities you can do in the community. Following are a few ideas that will not only benefit the community but you as well:

Teach a Class or Give a Demonstration

Community groups like women's clubs, garden clubs, the 4-H, and family clubs are always looking for speakers to share their knowledge with their members. You could speak on colors and how different colors on walls evoke different moods. Think about it. One will never see "red" on prison or hospital walls. Red is the color of aggression and has been proven to raise blood pressure. You could also teach a class on how to tape off door and window casings and show off all the products available for people who may be interested. Another suggestion would be to talk about the different kinds of interior and exterior paints and how to prepare the paint.

For these last two suggestions, you could also give demonstrations. Your local paint store would probably be open to your giving a demonstration if you will be using its products. You may also want to contact your local home improvement store. If it will help sell the store's products, then the store will more than likely be open to your conducting a demonstration. To help you, make a handout with some hints and tips that participants can take home. Remember to put the name of your business and your contact information on the handout, so that the participants can take a piece of your business with them.

Volunteer

Aesop said, "No act of kindness, no matter how small, is ever wasted." You may be thinking, I got into this business to make money, not paint for free. Volunteering, however, is one of the best ways to not only get involved in your community but also to build your business. While volunteering in your community, you will meet other people volunteering. Habitat for Humanity is a great place for a house painter to volunteer his time. Real estate agents, builders, plumbers, electricians, heads of corporations, and sometimes even mayors or past presidents volunteer their time to build homes for families in need. You probably won't get repeat business from the homeowner, but the exposure you get from working on one of these houses can be enormous. Many times, television stations will do a piece on the community work, and occasionally radio stations will broadcast their shows on location at the job site. You might meet a house builder there, or the plumber or electrician may know someone who knows someone. So, don't pass up volunteering your services.

Sponsorships, Donations, and Charity Event Contributions

Donate to local charities and other organizations. Typically when you donate, the organization will give your business some plug. It may be on a poster or in the organization's event program. Either way it is exposure for your business. In most cases you will be asked to give a monetary donation, but you may also be asked to sponsor a community softball or basketball league. This is great for you. Have T-shirts or hats made up with your company's logo on them. For an hour or more, four or five times a month, your company's name and logo will be out there in the community. You won't have to say a word. If you are too busy to physically work on a house, what about donating the paint for it? Charitable causes take any help they can get from any sector of the community, and most of the time these donations are tax deductible.

Publicity

Publicity is different from advertising in that you don't have to pay for publicity, while you do have to pay for advertising. Sometimes publicity can get you further down the road than advertising can. To get the publicity snowball rolling, you will have to write press releases. They are not difficult to write, and once you write three or four, you'll have the hang of it and will be able to whip out a press release in thirty minutes easily. We will cover that in this section.

Where most people go wrong with press releases is that they don't send them to the right people. For newspapers, magazines, or newsletters, you should send your releases to the editor of the publication. Station managers typically handle press releases at radio and television stations. If you don't send your press release to the right person, it can be discarded or left floating around in a stack of other papers until someone realizes it is in there. If you are not sure who should receive your press release, call up the publication or station and ask where you should send it. Keep a record of what you found out, so you will know to whom and where it should go the next time you send a release.

To get publicity you will have to show the media why your business is newsworthy. One way you are newsworthy is if you are a new business in town. Newspapers, especially the smaller suburban papers, like to announce new businesses and will typically publish an item about your business or send a reporter to interview you. Don't discount community newsletters, magazines, local TV and radio, and business and trade publications when looking for places to get publicity. They can be a viable market for you to break into as well.

To keep your name in front of people, you can write about a new painting service or write a new product review in which you give your opinion of the product much like a movie critic reviews a movie. This will only cost you your time and can lead to your being considered an expert in the painting field.

So now, about those press releases. It can be expensive to have someone write a press release for you, so you might want to tackle the job yourself. There's no great mystery. Just go with some basics, and you'll be fine. Check out page 162 for a basic press release, its form, and the information to include in it.

Photos

You may not have considered photos as being important in the grand scheme of your marketing efforts, but they can make a big difference. You can use photos not only when contacting markets for publicity but also in your advertising materials, and you will definitely want them for your website.

While it is always a good idea to have at least one good head shot taken of yourself at a studio by a professional, most photos you can take yourself because you will be taking pictures of your completed jobs. When you get your head shot done, get the digital version of your print(s). Today, that is how photos are sent and used. Very rarely is anyone asked for a hard copy of a photo because it will have to be scanned anyway to be made digital. When a hard copy of a photo is scanned, it loses its definition and can become grainy. Digital photos are easy to send via e-mail. All you have to do is send it as an attachment in an e-mail.

For job site photos, invest in a digital camera that takes pictures in high resolution. Canon, Sony, and Nikon are typically the best brands. You don't need to buy the most expensive camera, but don't buy the cheapest either. My digital camera cost around $450, and it is a workhorse. Check out prices, ratings, and specifications for digital cameras at www.digitalcamerainfo.com.

What kind of pictures should you take? To give prospective clients an idea of what you do and the workmanship you do, take before and after shots of your jobs. New coats of paint can give rooms an entirely different look. Show them off. You can use at least one set of before and after pictures in your brochure, but be sure to load all your sets onto your website.

Your Company Name

Contact Information

FOR IMMEDIATE RELEASE

Headline or Title (New House Painter in Town Brings Dead Houses Back to Life)

City, State, and Date-Month, Day, and Year. Your opening will begin here. Typically, you should put the who, what, when, where, and why in this paragraph. For example, "Two months ago, Dan Smith started painting turn-of-the-century houses that were being refurbished in the Historical District of Central Oklahoma. These houses are being restored because of their significance to Oklahoma's statehood."

The body of your press release should be no more than four or five paragraphs. Spend most of your time writing your opening. The rest of the press release will be used to expand on what you said in your opening. Reserve the final paragraph to tell a little about you and your company in two or three sentences.

At the end you should put your contact information.

CONTACT: Dan Smith

Phone Number

E-mail address

At the very bottom of your page, you need to center and type END or use # # # to indicate your press release has ended.

# # #

Advertising

Advertising is also a part of marketing, but it is a part you will have to pay for. You can typically find advertising methods that are easy on your pocketbook, but other methods can be very expensive. Take time to check prices and quality.

Weighing Your Advertising Options

While you are working on getting publicity for your business, you might want to consider some different forms of advertising. Before you decide upon this route, though, you need to think about how advertising will help your business and what you need to do regarding advertising. Following are a few ideas to consider before you get started:

- *Do you have a budget for advertising?* When you advertise, like networking, you have to stay at it over a period of time. Running one ad once won't do you much good. You have to keep your business name and contact information in front of people, so they will start recognizing your business and brand you as "the house painter in their area."
- *Will this particular advertising venue offer your business the ability to reach people who want your services at a reasonable cost to you?* You need to make sure your ad will reach people who want your services. If not, your money will be wasted. If you are paying $500 a month, but your ads aren't reaching potential customers or are reaching only a segment of that customer base, you might want to see what else is available.
- *Is advertising the only way left to reach your potential customers?* Have you tried networking and publicity? Because those two avenues of marketing are economical, make sure you have exhausted those methods of getting the word out before jumping into advertising. If you aren't seeing any results with networking or publicity, try doing a little advertising and see if that increases your business. Sometimes it just takes time to get people to recognize you and your business.
- *Are you expanding your business or moving into a new area like furniture refinishing?* If you are adding an extra component to your business, after sending out your press releases, you might want to take out a small ad to remind potential clients of your sideline.

- *Do you have your materials ready, and do they look sharp enough to compete with your competitors' advertising?* No matter where or when you advertise, make sure your materials look professional. Check for spelling errors and grammatical mistakes, and make sure you have the correct contact information. If you need to, hire a professional to put your ads together; just be forewarned that it could get pricey.

If you decide that advertising is the way you want to go, here are five suggestions to get the most from your advertising efforts.

1. **Set a budget.** A good rule of thumb is to set aside 10 percent from each job you do for advertising. If you make $4,000 a month, that's $400 that can be used to advertise the business and that money can take you quite a distance. Some avenues may only cost you a little bit of money. Others may cost you a lot. Check into all your options before settling on one. Remember, too, that advertising dollars are tax deductible, so keep good records.

2. **Determine your audience.** Decide early on who you are trying to reach. If you have put together your business plan, you already have a good idea. If you haven't, go to chapter 4 and look at narrowing your potential customers and devise a strategy to reach them.

3. **Put together an advertising strategy.** Think about what you want to do in the form of advertising. You might be networking and sending out press releases. Besides that, you could run a classified ad in one of the large papers in your area for a few months. This is doable. You are still meeting people face to face, but you are also letting people know you are out there ready to paint their homes.

4. **Put your plan in motion or take some action.** If you sit and think about what you are going to do, but never do it, nothing will get done. You may be busy, but by doing one task at a time, you will eventually finish what you need to do. For example, look on the website of the newspaper or radio station where you may want to advertise. Check out the ad fees or call the paper or station and have it mail you a fee list and deadline schedule. The next day, put together a rough draft of your advertisement or contact someone to do it for you. A few days later, contact advertising at the media outlet and send in your ad. Or you could simply take one afternoon out of your schedule and get it all done at once.

5. **Track your responses.** A good step to take is to test out certain forms of advertising for a few months to see which one will work for you. When you pick up a new client, ask him how he heard about you. If all you are doing is spending money and not getting any clients, stop advertising that way and use another method.

Even after the initial test, keep a number count as to how many people contacted you via a specific type of advertising. Flyers may work better for you than classified ads. Find one method that works and stick with it. See the Sample Marketing Report at end of this chapter.

Different Ways to Advertise

While there is no one "right" way to advertise, here are a few suggested routes you can think about taking. Check out all your possibilities and go with the advertising method you feel comfortable with.

Yellow Pages

One advantage to getting a land line for your office phone is that your business number will automatically be listed in the white pages of your local phone book. If you want to be listed in the local Yellow Pages under "Painters" or "House Repairs," you will have to pay for that listing, and sometimes those listings can be quite pricey. One plus about being listed in the telephone book is you will be where people are looking to buy "now."

A few cautionary words: Make sure that, if you decide to get into the Yellow Pages, you know which Yellow Pages you are appearing in. Never pay a bill to the Yellow Pages without checking the validity of the company and area of coverage. Yellow Pages is not copyrighted so anyone can use those words to suggest that you are getting in *the* Yellow Pages. Amazon lists almost one thousand Yellow Page books, including the *Jewish Yellow Pages, African American Yellow Pages, Golf Yellow Pages,* and the *Psychic Yellow Pages.* Since the cost is high to be listed, you want to make sure you are getting the most out of your money. Find out how many copies of the book were distributed in the past year—not printed, but distributed. It doesn't matter how many were printed, if they are not in people's hands, people can't find you. You will also want to find out what geographic area the book covers. If you live in the central part of your state and the book covers the northwest part, an ad in that book won't do you any good, unless you want to travel.

The following are five more points to consider regarding a Yellow Pages ad:

1. **Does your telephone company print and distribute the book you want to get an ad in?** If your telephone company does not print and distribute the phone book, you might not hit your targeted area if you are looking to get work from your community.

2. **How long has this book been published and how often is it updated?** You want to get your ad in a book that has some track record and is updated at least every two years. If the book is too old, people who receive it may not think it is very reliable.

3. **Does a book get into every household and business in your area or does it only go to businesses that pay for ads?** You are looking to get your name in front of every household that needs a paint job. Getting into a book that only goes to buyers of the ads will probably not do you much good as those people are looking for prospective clients as well.

4. **How many of your competitors are listed in the book?** If none of your competitors are listed in the book, there must be a reason. It could be because they didn't get any response from their ads. You can't afford to waste money, so if they are not listed, be leery. At the very least, ask around and find out why they aren't using this particular marketing device.

5. **How often do people use this book per week?** The company selling you this ad should have demographics it can show you on who uses its book and how many times a week they use it. Be sure to ask for this information before you give the company your $500 check.

Newspaper Ads

Newspaper ads can be effective, but they can also be expensive depending on where you want your ad and how often you want it to appear. The block ads spread throughout the paper can get pretty pricey. A good option is to put your ad in the classified section. Most classified sections charge per word, so you will want to make your ad short and informative. If you have a website (more on websites in chapter 9), it can work to your advantage here and really pay off. You can put the name of your company, a short and catchy slogan, your website URL, and a contact phone number. See the sample on page 167.

Smith Painting
Fast Service, Quality Paint Job
www.smithpainting.com
(800) 555-1212

Newsletters

Neighborhood or local home improvement newsletters might be a good venue in which to place a small ad. In some instances, you may only be allowed enough space for your business name and website URL, but if it will introduce you to customers in an area you want to work in, put your information out there. You will most likely only be able to find out about these newsletters through word of mouth, so keep your ears and eyes open. As an immediate source, check with your local real estate agents. They typically send out monthly newsletters.

Magazines

Check out local periodicals like community magazines and local business and trade publications to place business ads in. In Oklahoma City, I can think of three off the top of my head that are free to the community and almost everyone in town picks up. These can cost you a bit more because the magazine makes its money from its ads, but could be well worth it.

Brochures and Flyers

An 8½-by 11-inch one-page flyer or a one-page bifold or trifold brochure can help get the word out about your business. They are versatile and cost-effective since they can be used in a number of ways, from handing them out at meetings to mailing them. You can leave them with prospective clients, who can refer to them when they are looking for the services you offer. Unfortunately, most of these will go to file 13—the garbage—but once you get a standard format made, you will have a template to use in the future. These items usually contain a photo or a graphic and information about your business, like what services you offer, what you do, and contact information. You can make these pieces yourself using software on your own computer, have a copy center do it, or hire a professional. Of the three types, the flat, one-page flyer will be the least expensive.

After you have gained some clients, you don't want them to lose interest or forget about you. A newsletter is the perfect tool for keeping you in front of your audience. Newsletters have an advantage over flyers, brochures, and postcards, in that if you do your newsletter right, people will want to keep and hold onto the information you present. You can send a newsletter through the mail or post it electronically. Electronically, the cost is minimal because you won't have to pay for printing or mailings.

Newsletters don't have to be huge. One or two pages can be more than sufficient. It isn't necessary to send out a newsletter every month either. A good rule of thumb would be to send one out four times a year, at the change of the seasons. If you do that, you could cover what type of painting may be done each season and offer discounts on that specific type of painting. The following are some newsletter suggestions related to the seasons and beyond:

Winter

Offer to paint interior rooms like bathrooms, kitchens, and bedrooms so your clients can be ready for spring.

Offer suggestions on how your customers can start a budget so they will be ready to get their exterior painted in the summer.

Give some history of painting, write a review of a brand of paint, or choose a specific color and tell why it would be a good choice for a specific room of the house.

Spring

Offer reasons why a potential client should get the exterior of his house painted.

Offer ways a homeowner can spruce up his house himself, like painting exterior doors, mailbox posts, or window trim. You might think this is going against your cause to get work, but offering your clients ways to save money may just bring you work.

Offer a list of paints that can be used on exteriors, and talk about the advantages and disadvantages of each paint.

Summer

Offer suggestions on the best colors for house exteriors.

Give readers some suggestions for touching up corners, nicked places, and small paint repairs on ceilings or walls.

Do a little research and write about different types of woods used in homes for cabinets, doors, and bases. Write about the types of stains and sealers that are best for each type of wood.

Fall

Offer readers reasons to paint the inside of their home before the holidays arrive.

Discuss how wood can be cleaned and when it should be refinished.

Discuss the different types of surfaces, like concrete, masonry, and brick, that would benefit from a paint job.

Now that we have discussed certain ideas for a newsletter, let's discuss some specific aspects of your newsletter to pay attention to. Since you run a house painting business, you will always want to make your newsletter at least 85 percent about house painting and paint that goes on houses. You will want to focus on information your reader will find valuable and want to keep and refer to. Include an incentive for your reader to contact you, like a percentage off a paint job or a free estimate coupon. It's fine to list awards and achievements you've received, and if you are going to be doing a demonstration somewhere, be sure to include that information as well.

There are some specifics about the layout of the newsletter. **Choose a meaningful name,** one that people can identify your business with immediately. Also choose some sort of symbol so people will know from a glance where the newsletter came from. A good bet would be to **choose use your logo.** Your clients are already used to seeing it on your business cards or invoices, so use it on your newsletter as well.

Third, **choose a layout and design.** You need to decide how you want to present your newsletter. You will need a heading, issue number, and date when your newsletter was made. You can then put your information across the page, but think about breaking it into two or three columns. There are many sites on the Internet with newsletter templates. The full version of Microsoft Word also includes newsletter templates. If worse comes to worse, build your own by using the table feature in Word.

Fourth, **make sure the size is convenient and readable.** The simplest, easiest, and most convenient size to make your newsletter is 8½ by 11. It's easy to handle, and if you need to mail your newsletters, you can fold them like a letter. When you are putting your newsletter together, be sure to use a font everybody can read. Don't go too small on the type size, and don't choose a fancy scroll script type font. Not everyone can read these types of fonts. Times New Roman twelve-point seems to be the font of choice, although Arial or Calibri would work, too.

Fifth, **think about using color, colored ink, or colored paper.** Black type on white paper may be your first thought, but try to think in color. If you go with white paper, try using a different color ink in different sections of your newsletter. You should also think about using different color papers with black ink. You could go with green for spring, blue for summer, yellow or gold for fall, and red for winter. Pastels of these variations work fine. By using color, you will make your black type show up and the colors will get your readers' attention. You will also be color coding your newsletters. This will make your seasonal newsletters easy to find.

Sixth, **when possible use graphics or photos.** If you have a logo, use that in your newsletter. Graphics tend to draw in readers, and they are a good way to break up copy so your newsletter doesn't look like a dictionary. Even newspapers break up their copy by using big headlines and pictures. Pictures are a good way to spruce up your newsletter. If you are sending your newsletters electronically, pictures can give your readers a better idea of what you are trying to say in your copy, and they are easy to drop into your project.

Finally, **don't spend more than you have to.** Send your newsletters electronically whenever you can. This will cost you nothing but your time. You will have to print some to leave around and to mail, so either print these on your own printer or make a white copy and take it to a do-it-yourself copy shop. Figure out how many you need to mail and then print about fifty more to leave at places and hand out. I would start by leaving three to seven at various locations, hang one up on bulletin boards around town, and keep five or so in your vehicle in case you run across someone who might be interested. Don't overprint, but definitely keep one hard copy in your files and make sure you save a copy on your computer. Since you will be doing your newsletter seasonally, you may want to run more copies and replenish your supplies.

Be sure to keep track of how many newsletters you leave at various locations, how many are picked up, and how many contacts you made from them. By keeping track, you will learn which locations are your best outlets, which locations you can leave more newsletters than the bare minimum, and whether your hard work is paying off.

Now that you have your newsletter written and ready to go, to whom do you send it? You have quite a few options. You can e-mail it to the client list you have been building or add it to your blog. You can also make a place for it on your website and then put an announcement on all the bulletin boards you belong to telling people where to find it. You can mail it to your clients who aren't computer savvy or put it in the library, on bulletin boards around town, or leave some at your friendly local paint store.

For a one-page flyer, think about using brightly colored paper instead of the standard white. Bright colors will get the attention of prospective customers. Black ink is usually safe to use on all bright colors and will stand out on the paper. For a flyer, start out with a headline like "Need a Painter?" and then follow with a paragraph or list of the services you offer. You might want to say, "One Room or a Whole House—Interior and Exterior—We Do It All," if, in fact, you do. You will also want to say that you give free estimates and add all of your contact information, including your website. If you have any endorsements or testimonials, add a few to your flyer. Place them before your contact information. Three is a good number to use. To give potential clients an easy way to reach you, include tear-aways at the bottom or side of your flyer. These are small slips with your contact information so people can tear off a slip and take it with them.

When doing a brochure, whether bifold or trifold, you will want to include the information above, but you can add extra facts, like any certifications you may have or if you do lead removal or if you do furniture refinishing. You can include up to five endorsements or testimonials. In the beginning, you might want to make your brochure with colored paper and black ink. As you get more work and have more money to invest in marketing, move up to a glossy white paper and include color photos. Your brochures will cost more, but they will represent your business in a classy, professional way.

Before printing your flyer or brochure, think through all the information you want to include and put together a rough draft. Included in that information you will want to tell people how your service business is going to solve their problem or meet their needs. You will want to focus on the services your business has to offer as well. As an added bonus, you could provide potential customers an offer they can't refuse. For instance, you could include a coupon that gives 20 percent off to customers who need a paint job for a specific amount of time like from October 1 to March 1.

You could also do a purely informational flyer or brochure, in which you give people information about a topic, like what color can do for their moods. You could also write a review of the many paints on the market, letting people know what these paints can and can't do for them. These brochures are less likely to be thrown away because of the information included in them. You could take an 8½ by 11 piece of cardstock and make two flyers out of it by putting the information on the left half and then the same information on the right half and cutting the page in half. This would give you two flyers for the price of one.

No matter what style or size of brochure or flyer you choose, make sure you always include your contact information. You do want people to be able to reach you, don't you?

Bulletin Boards

Posting your business information on a community bulletin board is an inexpensive and easy way to get the word out about your business. You can find bulletin boards in Laundromats, libraries, churches, and some stores. You can put up your business card, a postcard, or a one-page flyer if there is room. Be respectful of where you are posting and ask permission to post your information. Most of the time, bulletin boards are open to the public, but there could be instances when the owner of the bulletin board has rules about what can and can't be posted. It could be as simple as allowing only business cards to be posted so more community businesses can post their information, so be sure to check.

Billboards

We've all seen those big signs glaring back at us as we drive down the highway. For whatever may be said about them, they do catch our attention. This may not be profitable for your business right away, but down the road, you may want to consider this form of advertising. Don't count out billboards as only for big companies. You can choose the size you would like to advertise on and what you want to say. Prices vary according to location, size, duration, region, and other factors, and can run anywhere from a couple of hundred dollars to tens of thousands. Lamar is the largest billboard company in the United States. You can check out its rates and what it has available by visiting www.lamaroutdoor.com.

Radio and Television

Of course, every business owner would like to be able to advertise on radio and television. The exposure can be long reaching, but consider the publicity route for these two markets before buying advertising time. Radio and television time is expensive, not including the cost of production for your ad. Advertising this way can cost you tens of thousands of dollars.

Vehicle Signs

An easier and cheaper way to get exposure for your business is to have your business name, phone number, and website URL painted on your work vehicle. That vehicle then becomes a moving billboard. Everywhere you drive, you will be exposing potential customers to your business. If getting your vehicle painted is not an option right away, get two magnetic signs with your information printed on them. Stick one on the driver's side and one on the passenger's side. You will still have the advantage of advertising, but if you decide to trade up in vehicles, you can just remove the signs and use them on the new vehicle. Magnetic signs will cost you about one-fourth of what you will spend on getting your vehicle painted.

Direct Mail

This type of advertising is mail that is delivered to people who receive mail from the post office. Typically this comes in postcard form or color brochures. You can focus your mailings by choosing which zip codes you want to target. Be aware, however, that most of this advertising gets thrown in the trash. To keep your postcard in potential clients' homes, try putting some informational material on it, much as you might do in an informational brochure. To look at pricing and check out your options, visit these websites: www.directmail.com, www.postcardmania.com, and www.postcardservices.com.

Yard Signs (at Work Site)

Another way to get cheap and easy exposure is to invest in yard signs. We are more typically used to seeing real estate signs in people's yards, but more and more businesses in the construction trade are using them. In the last few days alone, I've seen two, one for a roofing company and one for siding. You can find them in cardboard and aluminum. Aluminum would be the best choice because it would last for a long time through rain, sleet, and snow. They range in price from $40 to $80 depending on what you include on the sign. Check on prices from your local sign makers and compare them to an online company, such as www.yardsignwholesale.com.

Door Hangers

Another way to get exposure for your business is to visit every home and leave a door hanger. These are signs about the size of a brochure with a hole at the top so you can slip them over doorknobs. If you are shy and/or don't feel like talking to people, you can introduce your business to potential clients without ever having to talk to them. For these, you might consider putting your business name, phone number, and website URL on one side. On the other side put "Do Not Disturb." If people don't want to keep the hanger for the information on one side, they will probably keep it for the "Do Not Disturb" message on the other, and your business will have a presence in their home. Pay the extra money and get your door hangers laminated. They will last longer and make a nice presentation.

Premiums

These are items that you give away to promote your business, like pens, rulers, cups, writing pads, magnets, and more. They will, of course, include your business contact information and sometimes your logo. These are great to pass out at home and garden shows or networking meetings. If you are unable to attend an event, you can also send premiums to represent you, since they can be dropped into conference or event packets or bags. To find premium offerings, you can do an Internet search for "promotional business premiums." You will find thousands of sources to help you get started. As always compare prices. Also check out www.premsplus.com and www.nationalpen.com. They offer good products at competitive rates.

You may be dizzy from all the options, but don't think that you should use all of them. Choose the ones that you feel comfortable with and that will fit into your budget. You may choose to use one or two exclusively and the others never. You may want to try different options depending on your budget and what works for you.

To help you make better decisions on what is working and what is not, use the Sample Marketing Report on page 174. In the first column, you will write down the type of marketing you are doing—social networking, premiums, door hangers, flyers, etc. In the second column you will describe what that marketing includes, like "printed five hundred flyers, passed them all out or left at paint store." In the third column, you will write what it cost you to do that type of marketing, and in the last column, you will write the results you got from that type of marketing. Use this report as a way of tracking your marketing efforts. Analyze your data and use it to determine what steps to take in the future.

MARKETING REPORT

MONTH OF _____, 20_____

BUDGET_____

Type of Marketing	Description	Cost	Results

Comments: _____

_____

_____

_____

09 | The Internet: Addressing New Ways of Marketing

While home-based businesses are still going the traditional route when it comes to marketing their products and services, they are also using electronic media to reach potential clients. No matter what you are selling, the Internet has opened up not only local markets, but also worldwide markets, to people owning and running small businesses. Whether people use eBay or Amazon to sell their products or Facebook and Twitter to get the word out about their services, the Internet has created many ways for small businesses to succeed.

You don't have to have a big business to be successful, but you do have to be aware that you will have competition. As you read this, at least ten other people are reading the same chapter, ready to jump in and market their businesses as well. You may have an advantage in that you may be in a different part of the country than your competition, but then again, your competitor may be just a couple of miles away. What you need to do is get an online presence early and make sure that presence looks professional. With the cost of online setups pretty reasonable, you can get started right away. It may take time and effort on your part to learn all the ins and outs of the Internet, but as you progress, it will take less time, and your efforts will pay off.

In this chapter, we will investigate how you can get a presence on the Internet, how to get noticed, how to get listed in directories, how to find the best social networking sites for your business, and how to use them to your advantage. We will also cover what organizations to join online and how networking on those and other sites and exchanging links can be a win-win situation for everyone.

Building Your Website

You may be a one-man show and wonder why you need a website. The answer is easy—exposure. Consider it your 24/7 store that is open even when you're not there. But come on, what's the second-most commonly asked question after "Do you have a business card?" It's "Do you have a website?" And I'll admit it. I'm a website snob. When I hear of a new company or a person trying to sell me something, whether products or services, the first thing I do is check out their website. If they don't have a website, I have a difficult time taking them seriously. I know there are many businesses that don't have websites, but in today's electronic world, having a website is part of our business culture.

I know, too, that you may be thinking about all the work involved in setting up and operating a website, but it doesn't have to be a headache. All you have to do is break the work down into steps. Here are the steps you need to take to get your website going. At the end of this section, I have also included a worksheet to help you get your thoughts and plans organized.

Domain Name

First, choose a domain name. When choosing a name for your website, you should choose something easy to recognize, easy to spell, and related to your line of business. Sit down with a piece of paper and start writing down some names. Go with your company's name first—Smith Painting, for instance, but then come up with five or six more. The reason you want several options is that you have to see if the domain name you want is in use already. More on that in a bit.

Ask friends and relatives what they think about your choices and which one they think you should use. Is your domain name simple enough for you to rattle off to anyone? Can it be remembered, and can someone spell it easily?

After making your decision, go to www.register.com. Here you will be able to key in your domain name, see if it is available, register it, and pay for that registration. You can also use www.godaddy.com or www.networksolutions.com to register your domain name. Registration will cost $12 to $40 a year depending on the company you choose. You can also purchase packages in which your domain name is included in the web-hosting fee, and since you are just starting out, this is probably the way you will want to go.

While searching for availability, you will get assigned a three letter code at the end of your domain name. These three letter codes include .com (businesses and commercial organizations), .net (originally used for Internet organizations, but now used for businesses as well), .edu (education), .org (nonprofit organizations), and .gov (government). It is important for you to pay attention to these as you want your business to be in the right category. Since 80 percent of the top-level domain names use .com, choose your domain name with .com at the end. Your business will then be recognized as a business.

What if your domain name is not available? Go back to the drawing board. Come up with variations on your original ideas. For instance, instead of using smithpainting, what about qualitypainting, or ontimepainting, or pickyourcolors? Be creative with your name, but make it easy for prospective clients to remember.

Web Hosting

Second, you need to decide whether you want to build the site yourself or have someone build it for you. With so many options available today, I would suggest you try to build your website yourself. Many hosting companies like Register and GoDaddy offer templates you can use to build your site if you use their hosting services. Then there are websites like www.freewebtemplates.com, www.opensource templates.org, and www.wix.com that offer free website building templates. They are simple to use. You find the design you like, and then just fill in the blank or box with your information or drop and drag your information into the templates—easy for anyone wanting to have an Internet presence.

If you run into problems or don't understand the first thing about what the templates mean, you might want to sign up for a website building class at a community center, junior college, or vocational or technical school. These classes offer hands-on help, and the instructors can guide you through any trouble you may be having. Classes can cost $60 to $200 but are well worth the price if you need help.

Because you are not "selling" a product on your website, only conveying information, you don't have to worry about building a store and using enhanced security, so you probably won't need to hire someone to build your website. If you do hire someone, remember that it is going to be expensive, typically running from $1,000 on the low end to $5,000 on the high end. These figures do not include hosting fees and any other charges you might incur like upgrades.

Another idea is to find a computer-savvy teenager to build your site. If you don't have teenagers, check with relatives and friends. I'm sure some of your acquaintances know someone who can help you. Show him the template you like, offer him a couple of hundred bucks, and give him your content. Chances are he can have your site built and online within the week.

Content, Content, Content

Next you will need to decide what to put on your website. It doesn't matter whether it's a lot or a little as long as you have something up there. You will need contact information for sure, like name, address, office phone number, and e-mail address. On the front page or first page, you will want to put a paragraph or two about you and your business, a little about your background, why you started your business, and what your business philosophy is. You should have this information from your business plan back in chapter 4.

You will also need to include what kind of painting services you offer and maybe a one- or two-sentence description of what those services are. You might also consider putting in a little bit about your pricing, like "typically $3.50 a square foot." You could also put "free estimates" on this page instead of a price. This might also be the place to include a coupon offering 10 percent off on referrals or a particular service.

As you do jobs, take pictures of your finished work and put them on your website. Putting them up is not as difficult as you may think. Most computers these days have a place to save pictures. Once they are transferred from your camera to your computer, all you have to do is upload them to your website.

You will also want to consider including comments from your clients and customers. Ask if you can use their names when you load their comments. This gives the comments more credibility.

From the Trenches

If you make a personal connection with a client and your client loves your work, ask if you can get a recommendation letter or ask for a quote about the quality of your work and your integrity. You can use these quotes in your promotional material and the recommendation letters in your business plan. Referral letters are also useful when pondering the expansion of your business. Banks, paint stores, contractors, and other business associates can help build your business by telling others how you are to work with. Don't overlook getting these.

If you are going to be hiring employees, you might want to put your company policy manual on your website. That way potential and current employees can have the information when they need it. No more excuses that they lost their copies of the manual and did not know what was in the contents.

Don't be put off by the amount of content listed here for your website. This is what I consider the basics. Add what you can when you can. Many businesses get their domain name, put up contact information, and then gradually add other content as wanted and needed.

Keeping Your Website Updated

Once you get your website up and running, you may think you are finished with it. While it won't take you nearly as much time in the future, you do need to periodically update your site. It might be as simple as adding another picture or a comment or it could be as complicated as rewriting your opening/welcome page. Check your website at least once a month to see if all the information is up to date and add some type of new material. By adding new material, you are keeping your customers informed about your business and also allowing search engines to find you on the web.

Use the website checklist below to make sure you have everything you need to get your website going.

Website Checklist

- ❑ Chosen a name for my website.
- ❑ Registered my website URL name.
- ❑ Chosen a hosting site.
- ❑ Decided on a layout and design for website.
- ❑ Decided on content.
- ❑ Background and history of business.
- ❑ Company policy manual.
- ❑ Contact information.
- ❑ Description of what your business does.
- ❑ Made a "contact us" page.
- ❑ Photos of before and after jobs you have completed.

Getting Your Business Name Out There

Besides building a website, you will want to make sure you are listed on some online directories. In the old days, getting a listing in the Yellow Pages was essential for any new service business, especially for heat and air guys, plumbers, and landscapers because they probably didn't have a shop, office, or storefront location. Today, any listing is just as viable, but with the Internet, you have more options and more places to get your name before the public's eye.

While the Yellow Pages of your local phone book is still important, online directories are becoming more and more popular. As cell phones become smarter, more people, especially the younger generation, are turning to online directories on those phones to get information quickly. Being listed on these online directories can get you ahead of the game.

Getting Listed on Business Directories

These days you can find all kinds of business directories on the Internet. Do a Google search and you will find more than twelve million hits. These directories are like the electronic versions of the old Yellow Pages divided into categories. As in all things, there are some good ones and some bad ones, some easily searched, and some more frequently referred to than others. You want to find and get listed on the directories with the most traffic and the ones that will garner you business. Following is a list of some of the more frequently used:

- www.google.com/Top/Business
- http://dir.yahoo.com/Business_and_Economy
- www.atlist.org
- www.bizweb.com
- www.kellysearch.com
- www.dmoz.org/Business/Directories
- www.allconstructiondirectory.com
- www.industrialquicksearch.com
- www.b2btoday.com/bb/Construction/index.html
- www.anylistintheus.com
- www.business.com
- www.hoovers.com

Some directories charge you to be listed, much like the Yellow Pages, and others allow you to list your business for free. When you visit a directory's site, like B2BToday .com, at the top is a little tab that reads "Free Business Listing." Click on the tab and follow the directions to get your business listed there. Most directory websites will direct you how to get listed by following the link, "List Your Business." Be sure to include all your pertinent business information, and where categories are offered, investigate who is listed where so that you can place your business in the right category. It won't do you any good if you are included under "nail salons" instead of "house painting" or "construction." After you have completed the forms, be sure to check back to see that you have been listed and that all your information is correct.

Getting on Association Directories

If you don't belong to any associations or organizations yet, you need to think about joining one or two. One benefit of joining is that you get to be listed in their online directory. Your local chamber of commerce or small business association will no doubt have websites and list its members there. Sometimes groups like these feature their business owners on the front page of their websites. Be sure to take advantage of all the benefits these organizations have to offer.

If you join an organization, be sure to keep your information up to date. If your phone number or address changes, make sure to get that information updated on the organization's website. Typically, all you have to do is let the group know and it will make the changes for you.

Besides associations, you may want to be listed on some industry-specific websites. Since your service business falls under the larger umbrella of construction, you should check out the directories on the following websites to see if being listed there would benefit your business:

- www.thomasnet.com
- http://contractors.com
- www.homegiant.com
- http://directory.constructionjournal.com

Getting on Local Directories

While you may have been listed on the directories mentioned earlier, it's also a good idea to get listed on some local directories. The business and association directories will bring exposure to you not only all over the country, but all over the world. The same rules apply for local directories—make sure you are listed in the appropriate section and that all your information is correct. When you look in these directories, you will get a feeling for your local competition. Think about what you can add to your listing that will make you stand out or make your business unique. Sometimes, local directories allow you to add what your customers have said about you in the past. Be sure to include that information.

The following are seven of the more well known local directories:

- www.yellowpages.com
- www.local.yahoo.com
- www.citysearch.com
- www.jumptoyourcity.com
- www.insiderpages.com
- www.thewebmap.com
- www.local.com

Exchanging Links

Another way to get your business name and website out there is to exchange links with other websites. For instance, find a paint company with a website in your area. Contact the manager or the webmaster and tell him that, if he will list your website URL on his webpage, you will list his on yours. The more hits both websites get, the more beneficial it will be for both of you.

Be sure to add the website link in a timely manner. You could make a links page where you have all the traded websites listed, and when you add a new link, you could put a small announcement on your opening page saying, "New website link added."

Building Your E-mail List

At some point in your business life, you will want an e-mail list. It is better to start it sooner than to regret not keeping in touch with acquaintances, clients, business contacts, and friends two or three years down the road. By building an e-mail list, your business life will be simpler and you will be able to reach out to those people who you need to help build your business.

Getting someone's e-mail is simple: Ask for it. When you have it, enter it into a database you have built so that the e-mail address will be available when you need to contact that person. Another advantage of having an e-mail database is you can send out mass messages—announcements, coupons, or newsletters—to those on your list. This is a great way to keep in touch with people. When you build a database, categorize your information. Put a tag like "Client" at the beginning of all your client entries so you can search, find all your clients, and send promotions or discounts just to them. Place friends, families, business associates, and others into separate categories.

How often you contact the people in your database is up to you, but I'd send out something at least once every three months. This will keep you in their minds, and if you write a newsletter and do it correctly, the people on your list will start talking about you to others.

When creating a mailing list and sending out your material, always create an opt-out option for those who really do not want to get e-mails from you on a regular basis. Also, like your clients' phone numbers, keep this list to yourself. Don't sell the information, give it to someone else, or use your list for anything other than business. If you have personal information to share, separate your list and send that information to friends and families or those you know would appreciate receiving such information. In other words, be respectful of everyone's time and need to know.

Electronic Social Networking

You may think you are too busy to network in too many places face to face, but electronic social networking may be an answer to one of your problems. There are many social networking sites on the web, with the most popular being Facebook, Twitter, MySpace, and for businesses, LinkedIn. On these sites, people follow their friends, colleagues, and business associates. Word travels fast through these sites, so if you want news spread quickly, electronic networking is the way to go. When you join, people can sign up to follow you, so whenever you post a message, everyone who is following you can see your message. On Facebook, when one person signs on, she typically brings along her friends and relatives to your site. You can go from an audience of ten one day to five hundred or more in a month depending on how often you get on the site.

Social Networking Sites Where Your Business Can Shine

Today, you almost can't build a business without belonging to at least one social networking site. There are quite a few to check out. There are advantages and disadvantages to all of them, so you will need to decide which one will work for you. Here are seven of the most well known electronic social networking sites with a short description of what they are and how they work. There are others out there, so if you hear of one that sounds interesting, by all means, check it out.

- www.facebook.com—This site is where personal and business meet. When joining, you fill out a profile, tell about your business, sign on friends, and find friends to follow. You can post as often as you like. I would suggest at least a couple of times a week. Facebook has more than 500 million members so you will be sure to find friends to follow you.

- www.twitter.com—Twitter is similar to Facebook, but with a smaller user rate, currently 200 million. You fill out a profile and look for people or businesses to follow. The big difference with Twitter is you are only allowed enough space for 140 characters per message or tweet. If you own a Blackberry or an iPhone, this is ideal. You can get on, post a short message, and then get off.

- www.myspace.com—When you join MySpace, your profile becomes a mini webpage. As a matter of fact, some businesses use their MySpace page as their website. Here you can still invite people to join your site and post messages to those who have joined your page.

- www.linkedin.com—This network marketing site is where people go to get their business noticed and to get together with other businesses. There are more than ninety million members from more than two hundred countries. To join this site, you fill in a "company profile" and then communicate with those who contact you.

- www.myyearbook.com—This social site's slogan is "the best place to meet people," and with more than twenty million members, it might not be far off. Here you fill out a profile and then start meeting people. The drawback is that it seems very informal and many members go there to play the games the site offers. If you want to kick back, however, meet new people and relax a little, this networking site may be for you.

- www.livejournal.com—On this site, you can not only sign up, but you can also search for other social networking sites from here. There are more than thirty-six million users, and the site has news posted as well as a classified section where you can add information about your business.

- www.classmates.com—You never know who you will reconnect with on this site. Most people join to find old classmates they have lost track of years ago. If you are still living in the same area you grew up in, you might want to connect with people here.

Know that some of these sites have had trouble with privacy issues. While Twitter and Facebook are big at present and will probably be around a long time, other social network sites may come and go. New ones spring up all the time, and I'm sure in another five years there will be one that will surpass the current big two. Stay on top of the changes and give this new way of networking a try. You never know who you will meet, and any exposure for your business has to be good exposure. Right?

Face the Facts

If your schedule doesn't allow you to keep in touch with all the people you would like and need to, check into Constant Contact at www.constantcontact .com. This web-based program allows you to write one message and send it to all your contacts through e-mail, Facebook, Twitter, and more. No more going to this program and then that one. Consider Constant Contact your web-based one-place-to-send store.

Online Forums

There are occupational sites you may want to join that have bulletin boards where you can ask questions, post messages, and communicate with other painters. These are called forums. There are as many forums on the Internet as you can think of categories—car racing, genealogy, writing, raising children, politics, and on and on. And yes, there are even house painting forums. You might think at first that this is just a waste of time, but get one tip from someone in your field that will save you thousands of dollars or make one good contact and you'll think your time is well spent. One way to find these sites is to plug parameters into a search engine and see what comes up. Visit the sites listed and see which one is right for you. The top three house painting forums are:

- www.painterforum.com
- www.painttalk.com
- www.painting-forum.com

Like everything else, the forums have rules to follow. You will have to fill out a profile, and most sites like to keep curse words to a minimum. Forums have monitors, much like hall monitors from school. They keep a watch on what is happening in their particular forum. If things get out of hand, they will typically bar offensive people from the site or at least send them a warning.

The Dos and Don'ts of Online Networking

One advantage to these networking sites is that, once you post a message, it goes to all of the people who are following you or those who are on the forum, so you don't have to send messages to each person individually. While in one way, that's a positive, in another way, it may cause problems. Following is a list of dos and don'ts when you are networking online:

- *Don't vent online.* Even in the twenty-first century, we live in a small world, and with the Internet, that world has become even smaller, especially when we start moving in our own career spheres. If you say something online about another paint contractor or general contractor, paint store or client, chances are they may hear about it. If you are upset with a client or are having a problem and need to vent, do it far away from a forum, chat room, posting site, or your blog. If you have a problem with another paint contractor, keep it to yourself or know to whom you are venting. Make sure they are trustworthy and your rant will go no further.

    Venting online can cause a snowball effect. If you make bad comments about one client or contractor, people will wonder what you say about them and soon may start avoiding you. Of course, there is a big difference between venting and sharing your knowledge. Just make sure that it's the truth and not your opinion.

- *Don't post personal information.* Scary as the thought may be, there are people out there who may want to do you harm—stealing your identity, robbing you, or even stalking and killing your family. When posting on any public site, do not disclose your Social Security number, driver's license number, the year you were born, the place you were born, your children's names, or your spouse's name. Use common sense and remember that not everyone on the World Wide Web wants to be or should be your friend.

- *Don't send spam.* Nothing is more frustrating than getting information or requests you don't care to receive. On online forums, people have joined for a reason; don't post any superfluous messages. If people are reading your blog or newsletter, make sure they have asked to receive the information. You will not make friends or look professional if you send the latest joke you heard at the paint store to everyone you know.

- *Do be polite.* Rudeness, inappropriate language, and personal attacks will not make you friends or expand your client base. If someone comes on and says something that makes you mad or you are in a bad mood, it's best just to read the post so you know what's going on but don't post anything in return. Calm down, and once you decide how to be diplomatic and can be diplomatic, then post. You will not further your business by cussing or chewing someone out.

- *Do follow the topic.* When responding to someone else, stay on topic. If you have another topic you want discussed or covered, start a new thread.

- *Do say what you want to say and then move on.* Get to the point of what you want to say when you address a topic. Don't meander, talking about every little detail of your day or what you're doing tomorrow. No one cares. They want to hear what you have to say that is pertinent to the topic.

- *Do be helpful, not critical.* As my grandma used to say, if you don't have anything nice to say, don't say anything at all. If someone has posted about a problem, give him some advice or offer suggestions he might try. Telling him that what he did was the stupidest thing anybody ever did or that he totally ruined his home is not the way to go. Think about what you would do to fix the problem and then let the person know in a kind way. You'll get more bees with sugar than with starch.

Blogging

An alternative to a traditional website is a "blog" site. We've all heard of blogging, and basically a blog is a place on the Internet where you can have a forum to talk about any topic as frequently as you want with as much chitchat as you want.

Promoting Your Website and Blog

You didn't put your website up or start a blog for the fun of it or for your health. The point was to get people to go to your sites, so they can learn about your business. To get people to visit, you need to let them know your site and blog are available. Following are seven ways you can get people to go to your site:

1. Make sure your site is registered with the top five search engines—Google, Yahoo, Bing, Altavista, and Excite. People aren't going to know you are out there if they search for the name of your business, and it doesn't come up. To find out how to get better traction for your website, do a Google Search for "search engine optimization (SEO)." Through finding information you will learn how you can get your company's website first in line if a potential client is looking for your services.

2. Send out announcements when you get up and running and also when new, pertinent content is added.

3. Put your website URL and blog address (if you have one) on every piece of correspondence and business material you have—vehicle signs, business cards, invoices, newsletters, advertising, etc. If you put it enough places, people will check you out. Many times people may have good intentions and really mean to check out your site, but when they finally get around to it, they have misplaced your address. If you put your information on everything, they will be able to find you when they get around to it.

4. Create an e-mail signature that will go on every e-mail you send. Your e-mail program will allow you to make this "signature." When you write an e-mail, your signature will automatically attach itself to the end of your e-mail. You can include your name, business name, e-mail address, website URL, and any other information you want your clients to know, like your business phone number or business slogan. All this information will show up in paragraph form at the end of your e-mail.

5. Trade your business link with others who are in the same field—painting or construction. You will have to contact these businesses and ask if they will trade with you. Don't be concerned by those who turn you down; you will get some takers.

6. Link to both your own sites. If your blog and website are at two different places, make sure that your website URL is listed on your blog and that people can click from your website to visit your blog.

7. When visiting newsgroups and message boards, participating in chats, or attending online conferences, make sure your website URL is always attached to the correspondence you send. Get your name and your business known. When people start seeing you around, they will want to know more about you and what you do.

Today, blogs have become very sophisticated in what they offer their patrons. You have the opportunity to have your blog page be your website. You can add pictures, content, almost everything you can do with a webpage of your own. Blogs are generally updated more frequently, and you will definitely want to blog at least once a week to get your site on the blog's search engine. Check out Blogger at www.blogger.com to see what it can offer. You will still want to get a domain name, but you can link your blog to it easily. The great thing about Blogger is it is free.

Growing Your Business

There comes a time in every home-based business owner's life when he has to decide if he wants his business to stay where it is, if he wants to expand, or if it's time to call it quits. You may be fine with getting eight to ten jobs a month, with one or two employees including yourself, and not pushing any more. Perhaps you don't want to work extra hours to expand, and you'd rather spend time with your family or have your weekends off.

If that's your decision, that's fine, but more businesspeople we know get into business with one objective and that is to make money. To make money, you have to think about expansion. Making money is a big motivator to most people, and if you do your expansion correctly, you may still be able to grow and yet cut back on your time at work anyway. Perhaps you didn't have a choice about whether or not you expanded. Maybe when you started your business, it took off and grew at a rate even you couldn't anticipate.

So, now it's a few years down the road. You see your business differently. You want to go in a different direction. In this chapter, we will explore the pros and cons of expansion, how you could expand, bringing on a partner to help you manage operations, and when it's time to let the business go.

Are You Ready to Expand Your Business?

There are several considerations when thinking about expanding your business. While you may be pondering expansion to make more money, you need to be aware that expansion will cost you something in money, time, and your personal relationships at the beginning just as starting your own business did.

If you have been successful so far, maybe you have grown bored and want to do more. Maybe even try something a little different. Take the self test below before reading any further to see if you are ready to expand your business.

If you put a check mark beside eight of the ten statements, you are ready to move forward. If you only marked six or seven, you need to look at the unmarked statements and work on those areas to make your business stronger before expanding your business. If you only marked five or fewer, don't even think about expanding yet. You still have a lot of work to do.

Before you do anything, though, you need to look a little more closely at three areas of your business. They are mentioned on the self test, but because they are so important, it is prudent that you take some time to think about them in more depth.

Are You Healthy Enough to Expand?

If you are worn out or feeling sick or, let's face it, just getting old, now may not be the best time to increase your workload. Building your business took a lot of work; expanding your business will take just as much if not more. You need to be in good health and have the energy to handle the new challenges coming your way.

Self Test

(Put a check beside the statements you agree with.)

_____ 1. I am healthy and ready for a new challenge.

_____ 2. I have enough money set aside for expansion.

_____ 3. I have enough work for more than a year to hire more men.

_____ 4. I am excited and want to take advantage of the new opportunities around me.

_____ 5. I have new skills I want to incorporate into the current business.

_____ 6. I can stay focused on my business without destructive distractions overwhelming me.

_____ 7. I have the support of my family, friends, and working colleagues.

_____ 8. I have a clear vision of where I want to take my business.

_____ 9. I have written down the steps it will take to get my business to that next level.

_____ 10. My current business structure is solid and ready for expansion.

Do You Have a Strong Support System Behind You?

Is your significant other in the ring with you? Does he/she think expansion is a good idea? If your partner wants more of your time or is afraid you will be taken away from family time even more than you are now, perhaps you should reconsider. You will need and want 100 percent support behind you.

Do You Have the Funds to Expand?

If you plan on getting more jobs, you will have to hire more men and get equipment for those men to use. You will have to be prepared to pay wages, benefits, taxes, and Social Security. You may have to buy work vehicles, buy office space, and hire office help. In addition, you may have to give some of your workers raises and make them supervisors so they can keep an eye on specific jobs, or you may have to take on that role.

In all things, remember to count the cost.

Why Are You Thinking of Expanding?

Money is a good motivator for expansion, but you have to consider more than that. Are you ready to take on more responsibility? Are you thinking about building up the business and then selling it? Or has expansion happened over the course of several years and you want to get a handle on it? Have you been successful so far? If the business hasn't been going well, how do you plan to make a change successful?

If you have been a success—and success is defined differently for everyone—you may feel now is the time to move forward into other areas. Perhaps you have made a fair amount of money, but now you have gotten married, want to start a family, or need to start saving for your children's education. As a home-based business owner, you and you alone can dictate how much work you get, how many employees you have, how much hands-on work you do with the business, and how much money you make.

Perhaps you are focused on doing quality work and building your business with integrity. Or you like doing one job at a time and being able to feel the accomplishment of a job well done. Or maybe you have an artistic bent, really enjoy creating beautiful work, and now you want to do it on a bigger scale.

Whatever your motivations, make sure you have a solid fix on the goals you want to achieve as you expand your business. You should also take the following three ideas into consideration as you expand:

1. **Are you going to be able to stay focused?** Make a list of what you want to achieve and plan for the problems that may occur along the way. Changes happen in our lives, but we have to know which direction we are going to work through those changes. For instance, if you are in the middle of a nasty divorce, the timing may not be right to make your business bigger. Your thoughts will no doubt be scattered, and you need to be able to focus 100 percent on your business, not on your personal life.

2. **Are you and can you be flexible?** Small businesses can adapt and change much more quickly than big businesses and since you are the business owner, you can say what comes and goes with one word: yes or no. Being flexible as you build your business will be key to its continued success.

3. **Will expanding your business be fun?** Remember how enthusiastic you were when you started your business. You have to be just as excited about expanding it. You will need to carry that same excitement with you each day as you look at jobs, employees, and all the demands the extra work places on your personal life.

Around the Paint Bucket

There are times when even the best of us get discouraged with our work, but instead of thinking about the negatives, think of the positives of owning and running your own business. You set your own schedule, take off when you want, have the possibility of earning any amount of income you want, and can apply your own creativity to any job idea you develop.

How Are You Thinking about Expanding?

How you want to expand is just as important as why and when, because your decision will make the difference between a few minor changes or major changes. Perhaps you have been painting existing middle-class houses for years, and now you want to focus on historical homes as well. Or let's say you've been painting existing homes, where you offered bids by measuring the walls and floors with a tape measure. Now, though, you want to branch out and start doing new homes. With new homes, although the walls are up by the time a painter goes in, builders typically want their teams in place before construction even starts. If all there is on the site is a field, you can't very well measure walls. You have to know how to bid jobs from blueprints. If you don't know, learning how to bid blueprints is one step you have to take before you move your business in that direction. Vocational or technical schools and community colleges offer classes on how to bid blueprints.

Success Stories

"I was working as a salesman back in the '70s, but hated the income and the hours," Bob of G&C Painting in Oklahoma City said. "I started painting one house a month. That's all the time I could spend. As I picked up more house painting work, I cut back on the hours at the store until I could go full time. At one point, we were painting close to sixty houses a year. Last year, we cut way back as I'm close to retirement. But it was a good run when we were doing it."

Increasing the Number of Jobs

Maybe your expansion is more about numbers. Maybe you have been doing two houses a week, and you want to do four or five. This will require that you hire more men or you will have to work long into the night and weekends, so make sure you add that into your cost of expansion.

Perhaps you have heard about an opportunity with apartments or condo developments are going up like mad in your area and you want to get in on the action. Be sure that you think about the equipment you will need and the work involved. Most apartments have several floors. Will you and your men be able to carry your paint and equipment up several flights of stairs? There may not be an elevator available. Condos and apartments have high exteriors. Do you own a scaffold, can you rent a lift, or do you own one?

Moving Beyond Your Current Location

Size can be relative to your area. Maybe you are looking to expand your business into one or more towns or even states. If work is slowing down in one area or you have heard of great opportunities in other areas, you may be thinking about expanding your business there. It is good for growth, but there are several issues to consider.

Different towns and states have different requirements for contractors. You need to check into the permits, taxes, and employment requirements in this new area before you decide to move work there. A way to avoid dealing with all that is to subcontract your work under a contractor that runs work out of state but pays you from the state in which you live. You only deal with renting a location for a certain amount of months and doing the job. Freedom Painting did work in Colorado, Minnesota, Texas, and New Mexico for a number of years, traveling to those states for jobs but working under a contractor in Oklahoma and keeping Freedom Painting offices in Oklahoma. Even though Freedom Painting worked in another state, it was paid by a contractor in the state, so basically it was subcontracting from Oklahoma.

Your crew may not want to travel. If your employees want to stay in the area you have always worked, you may have to hire other employees to work in the new area of expansion. Remember to check the state and local requirements for employees. They may be vastly different for this new area. You may be limited to so many hours of work, pay more in the way of salary, insurance, and benefits, or need to have permits stating how many employees are on the job. You may also have to find a supervisor to oversee this new crew if you can't always be in the area to check on the jobs.

The cost may be too great. When thinking about expanding into a new area, consider how much it will cost you in the long run. With gas prices always on the rise, it may not be worth the money if all your profits are eaten up with gas expenditures. And if you are asking your employees to drive a distance or you are using company vehicles, you could rack up a lot of fuel expenses.

Help for When You Expand

You may also be able to find a student from a vocational or technical school or a junior college who can bid blueprints for you. That will be another person you can add to your team as you expand. Individuals who bid jobs are typically called estimators. The advantages to having an estimator is that the bidding process can be ongoing. While you may be able to bid only one or two jobs a week because of all your other responsibilities, an estimator can be bidding jobs all day, five days a week. You won't get every job you bid, but the percentages will be more in your favor if you are bidding more jobs.

If you are taking your employees with you on a job, think about what it will cost to house them, feed them, and transport them on top of their salaries. Sit down with a pen and paper, add up the numbers, and then subtract your profit. If you cannot clear at least 65 percent of your contract amount, don't try to expand far away. It won't be worth it.

Increasing the Number of Employees

Maybe you are at the point in your business when you would like to add some employees because you have picked up double the work you had a year ago. Before you hire anyone, you need to see if hiring more men is feasible—will it work in your long-range goals, how long will the work realistically last, and how do you intend to pick up more work?

Maybe you are planning to build a workforce of one hundred or more, so you plan to start small and add more workers each year. Do you have an estimator bidding jobs night and day? Do you have a contract to do three apartment buildings or an entire subdivision of houses with more contracted work down the road?

How will hiring more employees affect your current employees? Will they get more or less work? Will your current employees be able to get promotions and raises if you hire more employees or will your current employees stay in their same roles and possibly suffer cuts in hours and pay?

Increasing Your Services

Maybe up to this point, you have only painted exterior and interior flat walls, but during a slow period, you learned how to do specialty walls or you found someone who can paint murals. Now, you want to expand your business to include specialty walls. This is an excellent way to add to your business. While at first, it may not be a major income source for your business, it can grow into something quite profitable.

If you have a shop on your property, you might want to consider adding wood furniture refinishing to your services. Not only can this help in gaining clients, but you can also learn about the nuances of wood, what will strip old paint off, what should be painted, what shouldn't, how to repair wood, and which paint stains are best for each type of wood. This information will all help when you work on wood in the interior of a home.

Of course, you will want to get the word out about your new services, so be sure to tell people through word of mouth, online, and by any other method of marketing you may do. Take pictures of your new ventures and post them on your website. If people know you are offering more services and they have used you in the past and liked what you did, they will use you again.

Is Going Commercial Right for You?

You might not have ever thought about expanding your work into the commercial arena, but it is an option for painters. If you like painting houses, stick with it, but if you'd like to up the ante and are ready for a challenge, commercial work may be right for you. Commercial work includes hospitals, hotels, strip malls, prisons, convenience stores, office buildings, and more.

As in anything else, there are positives and negatives about going commercial. First, you need to be aware that most commercial work is bid off blueprints, and these days those blueprints are sent via the Internet. Make sure you are computer savvy before jumping into this field. Second, if the structure is new, commercial work has schedules that painters must keep to dictated by a construction company. With remodels there is a little more freedom, but not much. Third, more and more companies today want subcontractors to bond their jobs. This is like an insurance that states you will finish the job. That doesn't ensure that you will be paid, which brings me to the fourth point. You can make good money in the commercial construction field, but be prepared not to be paid for as long as forty-five to ninety days down the road.

The best way to break into commercial work is to meet with contractors, get on their bid list, and start bidding their jobs. You shouldn't pass up any house painting work at least until you have a good foot in the commercial door. Most people think you have to have a large crew to do commercial work. That is not necessarily the case. Freedom Painting can finish a six-story hotel in a month with a three-man crew. My husband's philosophy has always been "get in and get the job done." In his own words, he doesn't like to "mess around." Freedom Painting gets paid by the job, so he knows that the more jobs he completes, the more money he makes. He not only pushes his men, but he also pushes all the other subs around him. He wants them out of his way, so he can get his work done and move on. That's the way you should think about commercial work as well. If you like to take your time on a job, commercial work may not be for you. Fast does not mean a sloppy or poor job; it means going in, getting the job done, and not dragging it out.

Are You Ready to Add a Partner?

With your business expanding, you might want to think about adding a partner. It could be a good idea if you are picking up more jobs than you have time to supervise or you need someone to travel out of town or stay in town to watch over your interests. An added bonus about having a partner is that he will conceivably be as invested in the business as you are, so if you want time off, he can oversee jobs and the business while you are gone.

To choose a partner, look again at the information in chapter 2. Make your decision carefully and thoughtfully. After all you have built this business on your own. You don't want to take on a partner who can ruin a good thing.

> **Face the Facts**
>
> Set a steady pace for your business growth. You don't want to grow too fast. If you do, your business could implode. Since you have decided to expand, you obviously have had success, but if you grow too big too quickly, quality may suffer, customer service may suffer, and the attributes you became known for may be the attributes that bring you down. Set one-year, five-year, and ten-year goals for your business. Review them after one year and see if you are headed in the direction you desire. If not, you can always adjust. Your job will be to stay on top of things as you expand.

When to Call It Quits

As the old saying goes, "All good things must come to an end." How will you know when to close your business? You will feel it in your bones.

A good time to close your business is when you become bored with it. Once you quit growing in your work and it becomes more of a drag to get up and go to work, then it is best to start looking around for something else to do. If you don't like what you are doing, you are going to pass that feeling along to everyone else around you. Before the business you started gets a bad name, close it down and move on.

Another good time to stop is when you are ready to retire. Maybe you have built up your business and hate to close it down, but you and your wife have saved up enough money to buy a vacation home in Fiji and you plan on spending a lot of time there. If so, running a full-time business may be difficult for you.

You do have some options, however. You could pass your business on to your children if they are inclined to work in the industry. You could take on a partner or two as mentioned before and stay on as executive member in an advisory position, or you could sell the business outright. You could then start another business, put the money away in your retirement fund, or use it to buy or do something you've always wanted to do but never had the time or money to do it.

The third reason to close down the business is if, heaven forbid, you get in way over your head financially, you can't see a way out, and the stress is making you sick. You no doubt don't want to go out this way, but things happen. It would be better to close the business than continue to ride a sinking ship and possibly end up in the hospital along with everything else.

So work your business, expand it, but when you feel it is time to end your run, do so. After all, you wanted to start your own business so you could call your own shots. This is another opportunity for you to do just that.

Appendix

If you would like to check out house painting-related organizations, need to investigate government standards and rules and regulations, or want to find sources to continue your education, you will find resources for those matters and more in this appendix. While you may never contact, visit, or need all of these sources, you may find one or two that are invaluable to you.

This is by no means a complete list. Every day new books are published, new websites go up, and new information is assimilated into the world. My hope is you will take this information as a starting place and then build on it. Google topics you are interested in and see what pops up. You'll be amazed at the sources you will be able to find on your own.

Good luck and happy painting.

Web Resources

Business Owner's Toolkit

www.toolkit.com

On this site you will find the latest news on IRS requirements for your business. Also included are federal and state forms, legal forms, financial planning information, and a library containing business books. You will also find links to articles on starting a business, marketing a product, winning government contracts, managing business finances, internet marketing, and more.

National Clearinghouse for Worker Safety and Health Training (part of NIEHS)

http://tools.niehs.nih.gov/wetp

The National Institute of Environmental Health Sciences (NIEHS) is one of twenty-seven research institutes and centers that make up the National Institutes of Health and the U.S. Department of Health and Human Services. If you need information on occupational exposure to lead, asbestos, or chemical spills, hazardous materials safety and training or information on national toxicology, visit this website.

National Institute for Occupational Safety and Health (NIOSH)

www.cdc.gov/niosh

This organization is a division of the Centers for Disease Control and Prevention (CDC) and is designed to help prevent workplace illnesses and injuries through its recommendations and educational programs. On its website, you will find information on chemical, physical, and biological hazards and exposures on the job site, the latest news and updates on job site illnesses and injuries, publications, a resource guide, and information on research the organization is doing to make the workplace safer.

Occupational Safety and Health Administration (United States Department of Labor)

www.osha.gov

This website provides individuals with information on workers' rights, regulations for work sites, enforcement issues, data and statistics, training leads, and a link to file a complaint. A painting entrepreneur can learn a lot from this site, including what is expected of him in his work and safety requirements on job sites.

U.S. Chemical Safety Board

www.csb.gov

The U.S. Chemical Safety Board is a federal agency that investigates industrial chemical accidents. On its website you can read about what happened during recent accidents and how the accident sites were managed. You can also find the CSB's recommendation policy and recommendations in its reports on how employers can make the workplace safer.

Other Websites You Might Want to Check Out:

Historic Homes for Sale
www.historicforsale.com

Historic Properties
www.historicproperties.com

Old House Web
www.oldhouseweb.com

Preservation Directory
www.preservationdirectory.com

Advertising Sources

Association Directories
Construction Journal
http://directory.constructionjournal.com

Contractors.com
www.contractors.com

Home Giant
www.homegiant.com

ThomasNet
www.thomasnet.com

Business Cards
Great FX Business Cards
www.greatfxbusinesscards.com

Next Day Flyers
www.nextdayflyers.com

Overnight Prints
www.overnightprints.com

Staples
www.staples.com

Vistaprint
www.vistaprint.com

Business Leads and Tips

Business Network International
www.bni.com

Constant Contact
www.constantcontact.com

Digital Camera Info
www.digitalcamerainfo.com

Leads Club
www.leadsclub.com

LeTip International
www.letip.org

Electronic Directories

@List
www.atlist.org

Any List in the US
www.anylistintheus.com

B2B Today
www.b2btoday.com/bb/Construction/index.html

BizWeb
www.bizweb.com

Business.com
www.business.com

DMOZ
www.dmoz.org/Business/Directories

Google Directory: Business
www.google.com/Top/Business

Hoovers
www.hoovers.com

Industrial Quick Search Manufacturer Directory
www.industrialquicksearch.com

Kelly Search
www.kellysearch.com

Yahoo! Directory
http://dir.yahoo.com/Business_and_Economy

Forums
Painters Forum
www.paintersforum.com

Painting Forum
www.painting-forum.com

Paint Talk
www.painttalk.com

Local Business Directories
Citysearch
www.citysearch.com

Insider Pages
www.insiderpages.com

Jump to Your City
www.jumptoyourcity.com

Local
www.local.com

U.S.A. City Directories
www.thewebmap.com

Yahoo! Local
www.local.yahoo.com

Yellow Pages
www.yellowpages.com

Signs, Premiums, and More
4Imprint
www.4imprint.com

Direct Mail
www.directmail.com

National Pen Co.
www.nationalpen.com

Premiums Plus Incorporated
www.premsplus.com

Postcard Mania
www.postcardmania.com

Postcard Services
www.postcardservices.com

Sign Depot
www.yardsignwholesale.com

Social Networking Sites
Facebook
www.facebook.com

Linked In
www.linkedin.com

Live Journal
www.livejournal.com

Memory Lane
www.classmates.com

MySpace
www.myspace.com

My Yearbook
www.myyearbook.com

Twitter
www.twitter.com

Websites: Domain Name Registration and Hosting
Go Daddy
www.godaddy.com

Network Solutions
www.networksolutions.com

Register
www.register.com

Website Templates
Free Web Templates
www.freewebtemplates.com

Open Source Templates

www.opensourcetemplates.org

WIX

www.wix.com

Organizations

American Subcontractors Association

1004 Duke St.

Alexandria, VA 22314

(703) 684–3450

www.asaonline.com

This organization looks to support the subcontractor by seeking reforms against abuses by contractors to subcontractors, providing educational opportunities relating to subcontractors, and helping to develop better practices and services in the construction industry as related to subcontractors.

International Union of Painters and Allied Trades, AFL-CIO

7234 Parkway Dr.

Hanover, MD 21076

(410) 564–5900

www.iupat.org

The union represents more than 140,000 men and women across the United States and Canada working in the finishing trades. These trades include painters, drywall finishers, wall coverers, and more. There is a union fee to join and that fee varies from year to year. The website offers information on where to find a local union, government changes and updates, news and events, and more.

Painting and Decorating Contractors of America

1801 Park 270 Dr., Suite 220

St. Louis, MO 63146

(800) 332–PDCA (7322)

www.pdca.org

This organization can trace its history back to 1884. First called the "Master House Painters Association of the United States and Canada," it went through more than three name changes as it sought to stabilize its identity. In 1937, the organization became the "Painting and Decorating Contractors of America." Even though the name has changed, the organization has stayed true to its mission for its members—to provide "quality products, programs, services, and opportunities" for the growth and success of its membership. Besides offering its members support throughout the year, the organization holds an annual expo where its members can learn about new products, legislation, and other news pertinent to their business.

U.S. Small Business Administration (SBA)

409 Third St. SW

Washington, DC 20416

(800) 827–5722

www.sba.gov

Founded in 1953, this independent government agency has been helping businesses through business financing, business education, technical training, dispensing business information, and advocacy. It has offices throughout the country where a business owner can get help to start or expand a business. The agency also offers classes on business practices at different locations throughout the year.

Trade Shows

Conventions.net

18851 NE Twenty-ninth Avenue, Suite 700

Aventura, FL 33180

(888) 968–3944

www.conventions.net

Whether you want to attend a trade show or exhibit at one, this company can give you lots of information. Its website allows you to search different parts of the country to see what trade shows and conventions are available. If you want to exhibit, the website can also tell you where to get banners, tables, promotional items, and more.

Local Trade Shows

Check with your local chamber of commerce or visitors bureau for trade shows, home and garden shows, and conventions happening in your area. At these events you can meet new clients or find vendors from whom you can buy products, perhaps cheaper than you are paying now. You can also learn about new products and equipment in your field.

Marketplace Events
US Corporate Headquarters
Cleveland Office
31300 Solon Rd., Suite 3
Solon, OH 44139
(866) 463-3663
www.nationalhomeshow.com
This company organizes and promotes home shows all across the United States. On its website you can see a list of shows and sign up to exhibit at one if you desire. It has shows in Florida, Colorado, Iowa, Ohio, Oklahoma, New York, Utah, and Virginia at all times of the year.

Trade Show Directory
www.biztradeshows.com
This website is a directory of trade shows not only across the United States, but also the world. Don't worry about being overwhelmed. You can narrow your search by country, state, and what kind of trade show you are looking for, be it painting or the construction industry in general.

Educational Resources

The Faux Finish School
Louisville, Kentucky
(800) 598–FAUX (3289)
www.fauxfinish.com
This school started in the late 1980s and has grown to be the most respectable and most attended faux finish school in the country. It offers classes that range from learning sponge techniques to painting classical murals. Students can also learn the business end of faux painting.

Oklahoma State University Institute of Technology
1801 E. Fourth St.
Okmulgee, OK 74447
(800) 722–4471
www.osuit.edu
This college located in the eastern part of the state of Oklahoma offers an Associate Degree through its Construction Management and Trades Program. Here you will

learn the basics of construction in areas like plumbing, electric, masonry, and more. You will also learn how to bid jobs using the industry's latest technology standards.

SCORE (Service Corps of Retired Executives)

409 Third Street, SW, Sixth Floor

Washington, DC 20024

(800) 634-0345

www.score.org

This organization is a partner with the U.S. Small Business Administration. It calls itself "the counselors to America's small businesses." There are local offices across the country where you can receive business counseling. Online you can find forms for loans, how to write a business proposal, and take part in business classes that SCORE offers. When you start a new business, this organization is the first place you should go as the support it provides is immense.

U.S. Green Building Council

2101 L Street, NW, Suite 500

Washington, DC 20037

(800) 795-1747

www.usgbc.org

If you are interested in the Green Building Rating Systems or you are finding more of your clients or contractors are interested and involved in energy and environmental issues, check out this organization. They can direct you to where you can take courses and become LEED (Leadership in Energy & Environmental Design) Certified. This movement is becoming more commonplace and looked on favorably by clients.

Vocational Information Center

www.khake.com/index.html

Created and maintained by Kathryn Hake, this website offers vocational school information and advice. You can search for schools by state or by trade in areas like painting, masonry, carpentry, electrical, and more. Hake lists schools, apprenticeship programs, and other educational resources that will help you learn your trade and reach your goals. There is so much information and links offered here that in 2005–2006, the site was selected as one of the 101 Best Websites by ISTE Publications (International Society for Technology in Education).

Books You Might Find Helpful

Arnold, John, Ian Lurie, Marty Dickinson, Elizabeth Marsten, and Michael Becker. *Web Marketing All-in-One Desk Reference for Dummies*. Hoboken, New Jersey: Wiley Publishing, 2009. This book delves into building a presence on the web. It guides you through making a website, blogging, writing marketable e-mails, advertising, Facebook, and Twitter. If you are looking for an overall reference source for building your business on the Internet, this book is a good investment.

Garrett, Wendell. *American Colonial: Puritan Simplicity to Georgian Grace*. New York: Monacelli Press, 1998. This book takes you on a tour of several east coast homes and shows you the interiors of these homes, their colors, furniture, fixtures, and more.

Morrison, Hugh. *Early American Architecture: From the First Colonial Settlements to the National Period*. Mineola, New York: Dover Publications, 1988. If you are interested in early architecture, this book is packed full of drawings, plates, schemes, and all the basics for how they used to build homes.

Pittman, Rebecca. *How to Start a Faux Painting or Mural Business: A Guide to Making Money in the Decorative Arts*. New York: Allworth Press, 2003. If your talent runs to the artsy side and you can draw and paint, you might want to invest in this book. It gives suggestions for getting clients in a specialized market. Pittman shares her secrets for setting up this type of business, building a portfolio, estimating and bidding jobs, finding clients, and having them come back time and time again.

Other Books to Consider

Brown, Bruce C. *How to Use the Internet to Advertise, Promote, and Market Your Business or Website: With Little or No Money*. Ocala, Florida: Atlantic Publishing Group, 2011.

Dixon, Mark, with Bob Heidt. *House Painting: Inside and Out*. Newtown, Connecticut: Taunton Press, 1997.

Floyd, Elaine. *Marketing with Newsletters*. St. Louis, Missouri: EFG, 2003.

Lynch, Liz. *102 Secrets to Smarter Networking*. New York: Consult Ad Hoc Inc., 2003.

Smart Networking: Attract a Following in Person and Online. New York: McGraw-Hill, 2008.

Sansevieri, Penny C. *Red Hot Internet Publicity.* New York: Cosimo Books, 2009.

Sernovitz, Andy. *Word of Mouth Marketing: How Smart Companies Get People Talking.* New York: Kaplan Press 2009.

Index

About the Author

Deborah Bouziden has been involved in her husband's painting business for more than thirty years as she has pursued her writing career. She began writing and publishing magazine articles in 1985. She has published hundreds of articles, which have appeared in numerous magazines such as *Writer's Digest*, *Woman's Day*, *The Writer*, *Personal Journaling*, *Byline*, *Lady's Circle*, *ParentLife*, *OKC Business*, and many others.

Bouziden has spoken and held writing workshops throughout the Southwest for the Taos Institute of Art, Southwest Writers, National Association of Women Writers, Oklahoma Writers' Federation, and others. She has written and collaborated on numerous books and is the author of our own *Oklahoma Off the Beaten Path* and *Insiders' Guide to Oklahoma City*.

To learn more about Bouziden, her books, classes, and workshops, visit her website at www.deborahbouziden.com.